DISSECTING THE NEW *CogAT*®

FULL LENGTH TEST PREP WITH A PERFECT SCORER

CogAT 7 TRAPS AND PITFALLS AND HOW TO AVOID THEM

KAREN GE

 Aquahouse Publishing

Published in the United States of America by:

🏠 **Aquahouse Publishing**

ISBN: 978-0-9855068-5-8

Contact Publisher at:

aquahousepublishing@gmail.com

Printed at multiple locations worldwide

Cover Design by **Allen Zhang**

Disclaimer: The Trapdog in this book is a purely fictitious character. Neither the author nor the publisher thinks that he has anything to do with CogAT test designers or any other standard test designers. Whoever thinks otherwise is exercising his/her imagination.

* Cognitive Abilities Test™ and *CogAT*® are registered trademarks of Riverside Publishing (a Houghton Mifflin Harcourt Company).

Author and publisher have no association with Riverside Publishing.

Contents

Preface

Like millions of other children in this country and around the world, I needed a high CogAT score to qualify for special programs. CogAT is a group ability test that is widely used in the admission process of Gifted and Talented programs throughout the country. Across the border, it is marketed as Canadian Cognitive Abilities Test (CCAT) in Canada and as the CAT in the UK.

Unlike other tests, however, it's notoriously difficult to find test preparation materials for it. At the time of this writing, Mercer Publishing is the leading company that publishes full length CogAT practice test books. But each Mercer book contains nothing more than one practice test and its answers. As a test taker, I had questions like *what exactly is CogAT? what are its traps and pitfalls?* and *how do you avoid them?* I searched long and hard, but found no information that I could use. So I dove into research papers in educational psychology, especially those by Dr. David Lohman, the author of CogAT. These papers let me see CogAT through the eyes of its designers and helped me understand what they do to distinguish an able student from a less able one. To my disbelief, I found out that they would set up traps to make us test takers fall on our faces. When I navigated away from these snares in my own CogAT Form 7 test and got a perfect score, I was thrilled. I wanted to share my experience on CogAT with my fellow test takers so that everyone could benefit. After all, who knows the challenges facing the test takers better than a test taker? That's why I compiled my notes into this CogAT study guide.

This book is organized around each of the nine subareas in the newest CogAT Form 7. Each subarea starts with tips and warnings. While some tips are specific and aim at that particular cognitive area, others are more general in nature and can be applied to all the subareas. The tips and warnings are followed by a full length practice test for that subarea. The practice questions are carefully chosen to truthfully reflect the most common traps of CogAT 7. Finally a detailed explanation of each practice test question of that subarea is provided.

CogAT is a series of tests used to assess the reasoning and problem solving abilities of students from kindergarten up to 12th grade. Problems in each grade level have 50% overlap with those in adjacent levels but become harder and harder as you move up through the levels. As documented in Dr. Lohman's papers, however, the basic thinking behind this test sequence is the same. So anyone who is preparing for the CogAT test would benefit from this book. That being said, I feel that this book is particularly relevant to students 3rd grade and above (Levels 10 – 17/18 in CogAT Form 7).

Karen Ge

Lisle, Illinois

Introduction

First, there are two "characters" in this book that you should know about. One is ... the CogAT Cat! You met him in the Preface already. This friendly cat will guide you through this book giving you tips and warnings about the CogAT test. You should listen to these pieces of advice because they will help you A LOT!

Hello! I'm the CogAT Cat and I'm here to help you prepare for the CogAT test!

The other is ... the Trapdog. Dun, dun, dun, DUN!! This fellow has a mean streak and it shows! Basically the Trapdog wants you to get in trouble. He's the guy to watch out for. He tries to undermine all the things that will help you get a perfect score. Oh no! Here he comes!

HA HA! You can't outsmart me, little test taker! I'm going to mess you up good, unless that little cat messes *me* up...

Avoid the Trapdog, remember what the CogAT Cat says, and you'll pass the CogAT with flying colors!

Part One

Verbal

Chapter 1

Verbal Analogies Traps and Tips

Do you sometimes circle an answer before reading through all the answer choices in a multiple choice test? If the answer is yes, you are not alone. Many people are like that, especially younger children. Don't cling to the wishful thinking that the Trapdog does not know your little secret. He does. It is stated plain and clear in <u>CogAT Practice Activities Teacher Guide</u> that "Students might select an answer choice before checking all the answers." The Trapdog certainly would not let this wonderful opportunity go by. His strategy in such situations is to set up distracters to fool you away from the right answer choice. I am sorry to tell you but this trap works again and again.

You youngsters fall for this every time! You have no patience, and that'll cost you dearly!! A little bait will be the end of you! Mwua ha ha ha!!!

It takes practice, but this trap is not unavoidable. What I did during my own CogAT test was that I kept on telling myself silently to manage my impulsivity and check all the answers. If you would like to learn more about how to do it, I recommend "Training impulsive children to talk to themselves" by Meichenbaum and Goodman.*

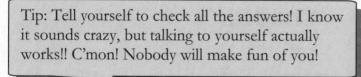

Tip: Tell yourself to check all the answers! I know it sounds crazy, but talking to yourself actually works!! C'mon! Nobody will make fun of you!

Now let's look at the first part of verbal reasoning: verbal analogies. For verbal analogies, the right answer is the one that makes the most sense. Watch out for what part of speech the words are! Noun should match noun; verb should match verb, etc. If the part of speech isn't right, you will waste precious time trying to do the analogy the wrong way.

Look out for the Trapdog!! He's waiting for you to pick the wrong part of speech! Don't be fooled!

First let's look at this analogy:

1. TV → watch : newspaper →

A. deliver   B. comics   C. read   D. magazine   E. listen

* Meichenbaum, D. H., & Goodman, J. (1971). Training impulsive children to talk to themselves: A means of developing self-control. Journal of Abnormal Psychology, 77 (pp. 115–126).

You might think: Well, a newspaper is *delivered*. A newspaper contains *comics*. People *read* newspaper. Newspaper and *magazine* are both periodicals. Watch and *listen* are both verbs.

When you think in these lines, you are very close to becoming the prey of the Trapdog. So stop yourself immediately and use logic instead.

Now you think: *TV* is to *watch* as *newspaper* is to what? That word must be a verb because you watch TV and *watch* is a verb. So now you can eliminate answer choices B and D because they are nouns. Next you can eliminate Answer E because you do not *listen* to a newspaper. So you have only Answer A. *deliver* and Answer C. *read* left.

Finally, you read the analogy one more time and decide which is better: *TV* is to *watch* as *newspaper* is to *deliver;* or, *TV* is to *watch* as *newspaper* is to *read*. The latter sounds better because most people watch TV and read newspaper, but not that many people deliver newspaper.

So your final choice is Answer C. *read*. Congratulations! You were not fooled by related words. Instead, you used your brain and made a logical choice.

Now let's take a look at another example.

2. cook → stove : wash →

J. hands   K. food   L. sink   M. kitchen   N. oven

> Tip: For verbal analogies, make a bridge sentence! Use logic instead of association!

One important thing about verbal analogies is that you should make a **bridge sentence** to connect the first pair of words so that it makes sense. Furthermore, this bridge should apply similarly to the second pair of words. Here, for example, you might use "a cook uses a stove" as a bridge sentence for the first pair. But this bridge doesn't really work because *wash*, the counterpart of *cook* in the second pair, is not a noun. Don't be discouraged if your initial bridge doesn't work. It's an important first step! A better bridge might be "we use a stove to cook." Now to solve the analogy, you only need to answer this question: what do we use to wash?

Answers K, M, and N are now eliminated immediately because we do not use *food*, *kitchen*, or *oven* to wash. Next you check which is better: we use a *stove* to *cook;* we use *hands* to *wash*. Or, we use a *stove* to *cook;* we use a *sink* to *wash*. Here *stove* and *sink* are both appliances, but *hands* are not. **So you choose L. *sink*.** Congratulations! You are right.

* Costa, A. (2001) Habits of Mind. In A. Costa, (Ed.) *Developing Minds: A Resource Book for Teaching Thinking*, Alexandria, VA: Association for Supervision and Curriculum Development (pp. 80–86).

Chapter 2

Verbal Analogies Practice Test

(24 questions, 10 minutes)

In the Verbal Analogies subtest, students are given a pair of words and another word without its pair. The first pair of words is related in some way. Students must determine how they are related and then select the word from the available answers that has the same relationship with the third word.

1. tomorrow → yesterday : yet →

A. until   B. after   C. before   D. already   E. today

2. week → month : yard →

J. day   K. mile   L. inch   M. year   N. distance

3. jump → hop : run →

A. leap   B. walk   C. jog   D. gallop   E. bounce

4. cat → claws : person →

J. teeth   K. feet   L. fingernails   M. hands   N. hair

5. runner → run : ballerina →

A. ballet   B. somersault   C. gymnast   D. dance   E. tutu

6. our → hour : their →

J. them   K. tear   L. rear   M. there   N. they

7. distance → mile : time →

A. clock   B. midnight   C. hour   D. inch   E. sunrise

8. bounce → ball : hop →

J. baseball   K. baby   L. pig   M. kangaroo   N. jump

9. wrote → write : read →

A. book   B. written   C. road   D. read   E. recite

10. son → mother : mother →

J. daughter   K. father   L. wife   M. grandfather   N. grandmother

11. school → fish : class →

A. students   B. principal   C. water   D. teacher   E. group

12. July → January : winter →

J. spring   K. month   L. summer   M. season   N. autumn

13. bear → paw : horse →

A. foot   B. paw   C. horseshoe   D. foal   E. hoof

14. musician → entertainment : teacher →

J. students   K. school   L. homework   M. instruction   N. principal

15. food → hunger : water →

A. element   B. drink   C. starvation   D. liquid   E. thirst

16. light bulb → electricity : car →

J. oil   K. motor   L. wheels   M. generator   N. gasoline

17. preacher → teacher : flawed →

A. damaged   B. clawed   C. perfect   D. student   E. fail

18. smile → happiness : frown →

J. worry   K. terror   L. mood   M. temper   N. fury

19. Tuesday → Friday : Saturday →

A. Monday   B. Tuesday   C. Wednesday   D. Thursday   E. Weekend

20. classroom → teacher : courtroom →

J. police officer   K. criminal   L. judge   M. witness   N. reporter

21. weed → pull out : error →

A. push in   B. correct   C. flower   D. mistake   E. erase

22. reptile → snake : bird →

J. nest   K. animal   L. feather   M. egg   N. robin

23. meter → centimeter : century →

A. day   B. month   C. year   D. decade   E. millennium

24. mitt → baseball : web →

J. spider   K. catch   L. ball   M. internet   N. fly

STOP

Verbal Battery Bubble Form

Verbal Analogies

1 (A) (B) (C) (D) (E)
2 (J) (K) (L) (M) (N)
3 (A) (B) (C) (D) (E)
4 (J) (K) (L) (M) (N)
5 (A) (B) (C) (D) (E)
6 (J) (K) (L) (M) (N)
7 (A) (B) (C) (D) (E)
8 (J) (K) (L) (M) (N)
9 (A) (B) (C) (D) (E)
10 (J) (K) (L) (M) (N)
11 (A) (B) (C) (D) (E)
12 (J) (K) (L) (M) (N)
13 (A) (B) (C) (D) (E)
14 (J) (K) (L) (M) (N)
15 (A) (B) (C) (D) (E)
16 (J) (K) (L) (M) (N)
17 (A) (B) (C) (D) (E)
18 (J) (K) (L) (M) (N)
19 (A) (B) (C) (D) (E)
20 (J) (K) (L) (M) (N)
21 (A) (B) (C) (D) (E)
22 (J) (K) (L) (M) (N)
23 (A) (B) (C) (D) (E)
24 (J) (K) (L) (M) (N)

Sentence Completion

1 (A) (B) (C) (D) (E)
2 (J) (K) (L) (M) (N)
3 (A) (B) (C) (D) (E)
4 (J) (K) (L) (M) (N)
5 (A) (B) (C) (D) (E)
6 (J) (K) (L) (M) (N)
7 (A) (B) (C) (D) (E)
8 (J) (K) (L) (M) (N)
9 (A) (B) (C) (D) (E)
10 (J) (K) (L) (M) (N)
11 (A) (B) (C) (D) (E)
12 (J) (K) (L) (M) (N)
13 (A) (B) (C) (D) (E)
14 (J) (K) (L) (M) (N)
15 (A) (B) (C) (D) (E)
16 (J) (K) (L) (M) (N)
17 (A) (B) (C) (D) (E)
18 (J) (K) (L) (M) (N)
19 (A) (B) (C) (D) (E)
20 (J) (K) (L) (M) (N)

Verbal Classification

1 (A) (B) (C) (D) (E)
2 (J) (K) (L) (M) (N)
3 (A) (B) (C) (D) (E)
4 (J) (K) (L) (M) (N)
5 (A) (B) (C) (D) (E)
6 (J) (K) (L) (M) (N)
7 (A) (B) (C) (D) (E)
8 (J) (K) (L) (M) (N)
9 (A) (B) (C) (D) (E)
10 (J) (K) (L) (M) (N)
11 (A) (B) (C) (D) (E)
12 (J) (K) (L) (M) (N)
13 (A) (B) (C) (D) (E)
14 (J) (K) (L) (M) (N)
15 (A) (B) (C) (D) (E)
16 (J) (K) (L) (M) (N)
17 (A) (B) (C) (D) (E)
18 (J) (K) (L) (M) (N)
19 (A) (B) (C) (D) (E)
20 (J) (K) (L) (M) (N)

Chapter 3

Verbal Analogies Test Solutions

I recommend that you read through these solutions carefully even when you get the right answer. They might give you some insight into how to solve real CogAT problems.

1. This question tests opposite relationships. *Tomorrow* is the future, and *yesterday* is the past. So they are opposite to each other. Then what is the opposite of *yet*? *Yet* is something that has not happened, so the opposite of it should be something that has happened. Thus Answers A, B, and E are all ruled out because they are not the opposite of *yet*. Now we are left with Answers C. *before* and D. *already*. Let's see which is better: *tomorrow* is to *yesterday* as *yet* is to *before*; or, *tomorrow* is to *yesterday* as *yet* is to *already*? Here *already* makes sense, but *before* does not sound quite right because its opposite is *after*, not *yet*. **So Answer D. *already* is the right answer.**

2. This question tests degrees. *Week* and *month* are both measurements of time but each month has multiple weeks. So the question now is: what answer choice is a multiple of a *yard*? Clearly Answers J and M are not multiples of a *yard*. Answer L is not correct because an *inch* is a fraction of a *yard*, not a multiple of it. Answer N is not correct because *yard* is a measurement of *distance* and *distance* is a group that contains *yard*. **Only Answer K. *mile* is a multiple of yard and it is the right answer.**

3. Again this question tests degrees. *Hop* is a small *jump*. So now the question is: what is *run* in a smaller degree? Answers A and E are ruled out because *leap* and *bounce* are not running. Answer D is incorrect because *gallop* is even faster than *run*. So we have B. *walk* and C. *jog* left. We see that C. *jog* is a better choice because it is running in a smaller degree and *walk* is not running at all. **So Answer C. *jog* is the right answer.**

4. This question tests part and whole relationship. *Claws* are a part of a *cat*. Clearly all the answers are parts of a person. Then we have to ask ourselves

a further question: what part of a *person* plays a similar role as *claws* do to a *cat*? Now we can rule out Answer N because *hair* doesn't function like *claws*. Answer J. *teeth* is not correct because *claws* are not used to eat. We also see that K. *feet* and M. *hands* are incorrect because their corresponding body parts in a cat are the paws, not *claws*. **So L. *fingernails* is the right answer.**

5. This question tests the relationship between a subject and its action. One bridge sentence for the first pair might be: a runner runs. Now the question to ask is: what does a ballerina do? Here we can eliminate Answers C and E because they are not actions of a ballerina. We can also eliminate Answer B. *somersault* because that's not what a ballerina does most of the time. So now we have only Answers A. *ballet* and D. *dance* left. It's tempting to say that *runner* is to *run* as *ballerina* is to *ballet*. It sounds good but it's incorrect because *ballet* is not a verb. **So the right answer is Answer D. *dance*.**

6. This question tests homophones. *Our* has the same pronunciation as *hour*. So we need to find a word that is pronounced exactly like *their*. **So Answer M. *there* is the correct answer.**

7. This question tests member and group relationship. A bridge sentence might be: *Mile* is a measure of *distance*. Now we only need to answer this question: what is a measure of *time*? Here we can rule out Answers B and E because *midnight* and *sunrise* are particular moments of *time* instead of measures of *time*. Answer D is not correct because *inch* is a measure of length, not time. Answer A is incorrect because although *clock* tells us time, it does not measure time itself. **So the only answer left, C. *hour*, is the right answer.**

8. This question tests a subject and its action. A bridge sentence might be: a *ball bounces*. Now let's ask ourselves this: what object *hops*? First Answer N. *jump* can be ruled out because it is not an object. We can also rule out Answers K and L because *baby* and *pig* do not usually hop. Answer J is incorrect because a *baseball* could bounce but not hop. **So M. *kangaroo* is the right answer.**

9. This question tests a verb and its tenses. *Wrote* is the past tense of *write*. So the question now is: *read* is the past tense of what verb? The answer is *read*. **So Answer D. *read* is the right answer.**

10. This question tests the relationship between generations. In the first pair, *son* is one generation younger than *mother*. So in the second pair the right answer

should be one generation older than *mother*. So we can rule out Answers J, K, and L. Now let's see which is better: *son* is to *mother* as *mother* is to *grandfather*; or, *son* is to *mother* as *mother* is to *grandmother*? Since *son* and *mother* belong to different genders, the right answer should also belong to a gender that is different from that of a mother. **So M. *grandfather* is the right answer.**

11. This question tests member and group relationship. Let's ask ourselves: a *school* of *fish* corresponds to a *class* of what? Clearly Answers B and D are not correct because they are singular nouns. Answers C and E are not correct because we do not say a class of *water*, or a class of *group*. **So A. *students* is the right answer.**

12. This question tests opposite relationships. *July* and *January* are six months apart. They represent opposite seasons. So now the question is: what is the opposite of *winter*? **The right answer is L. *summer*.**

13. This question tests part and whole relationship. *Bear* has *paws*. Now the question is: what part of a *horse* is like a *paw* to a *bear*? Answer D can be eliminated because a *foal* is an offspring of a horse, not a body part of a horse. Answer C is incorrect because *horseshoe* is not a natural part of a horse like a bear's paw. Answers A and B are not correct because we don't say the *foot* of a horse, or the *paw* of a horse. **Therefore, the only answer left, Answer E. *hoof*, is the right answer.**

14. This question tests people and things they do. A bridge sentence might be: a *musician* provides *entertainment*. So the question now is: what does a *teacher* provide? Answers J, K, and N can be ruled out because they are not the things a teacher provides. Answer L is incorrect because a teacher provides *homework* some but not all the time. **So M. *instruction* is the right answer.**

15. This question tests sequences. A bridge sentence might be: *hunger* makes people seek *food*. Now let's ask ourselves: what makes people seek *water*? Answers A, B, and D do not fit our bridge sentence well. For example, we do not say *drink makes people seek water*. So now we only have Answers C. *starvation* and E. *thirst* left. Answer C is incorrect because *starvation* makes people seek food more than water. **So Answer E. *thirst* is the right answer.**

16. This question tests the relationship between two objects. A bridge sentence might be: *light bulb* consumes *electricity*. Now the question is: what does a *car*

consume? Answers K, L, and M can be ruled out because they are not consumed by a car. Answer J is incorrect because a car doesn't consume *oil* the way *electricity* is consumed by *light bulb*. **Therefore N. *gasoline* is the right answer.**

17. This question tests rhyming words. *Preacher* rhymes with *teacher*. *Flawed* rhymes with *clawed*. **So the right answer is B. *clawed*.**

18. This question tests the relationship between people's emotion and facial expression. A bridge sentence might be: *happiness* makes people *smile*. Now the question is: what emotion makes people *frown*? Answer L can be eliminated because *mood* is a general term of all emotions instead of one specific emotion. Answers K, M, and N can be ruled out too because *terror, temper,* or *fury* causes stronger facial expressions in people than just frowning. **So Answer J. *worry* is the right answer.**

19. This question tests order of the days. A bridge sentence might be: *Friday* is three days after *Tuesday*. So the question is: what day is three days after *Saturday*? **The right answer is B. *Tuesday*.**

20. This question tests people and the place associated with them. Let's ask ourselves this question: *classroom* is to *teacher* as *courtroom* is to whom? Answers J, K, and N can be ruled out because *police officer, criminal,* and *reporter* are not in the courtroom most of the time. Answer M can be ruled out also because the role a *witness* plays in a courtroom is not quite like the role a teacher plays in a classroom. **So L. *judge* is the right answer.**

21. This question tests action and the object of the action. Let's see: weed is to *pull out* as *error* is to what? Answers C and D can be ruled out because *pull out* is a verb, but *flower* and *mistake* are not verbs. Answer A can be ruled out because we do not *push in* an error. So now we only have Answers B and E left. Now let's see which is better: *weed* is to *pull out* as *error* is to *correct;* or, *weed* is to *pull out* as *error* is to *erase*? Either is fine, only that when we pull out a weed, we have not corrected it yet. **So E. *erase* is the best answer.**

22. This question tests member and group relationship. A bridge sentence might be: *snake* is a *reptile*. Now we ask: what is a *bird*? Answers J, L, and M can be ruled out because *nest, feather,* and *egg* are not birds. Answer K is incorrect because an *animal* is not necessarily a bird. **So Answer N. *robin* is the right answer.**

23. This question tests degrees. A bridge sentence might be: one *meter* is 100 times of a *centimeter*. So the question we want to ask ourselves is: one *century* is 100 times of what? The answer is year. **So Answer C. *year* is the right answer.**

24. This question tests objects and their purposes. A bridge sentence might be: *mitt* is used to catch *baseball*. So now we ask: *web* is used to catch what? Answer K can be ruled out because *baseball* is a noun but *catch* is a verb. Answers J, L, and M can be ruled out because *web* is not used to catch *spider*, *ball*, or *internet*. **So Answer N. *fly* is the right answer.**

Chapter 4

Sentence Completion Traps and Tips

In his paper "Beliefs about Ability and Accomplishment,"* Dr. Lohman wrote, "[M]ost third graders can easily read the sentence *Cats have two eyes but only one _____*. However, some select a foil such as *ears* because they make inferences associatively rather than logically." Please read this quoted text **three** more times because it highlights the ultimate trap in CogAT Verbal Reasoning!

I bet you'll think associatively rather than logically. Mwua ha ha! DO IT!!

Watch out for this trap! **Do not** think associatively (ooh, this is related to that! I'll choose it). Think logically!

* Lohman, D. F. (2006). Beliefs about differences between ability and accomplishment: From folk theories to cognitive science. Roeper Review, 29 (pp. 32–40).

In the same paper, Dr. Lohman wrote, "[The sentence completion test] is probably the oldest and still one of the best formats for measuring verbal reasoning abilities. It focuses on the central task [of] verbal comprehension: making inferences about the meaning of unknown words or incompletely spoken language."

Indeed, Dr. Lohman seems to be fond of sentence completion. When the newest CogAT Form 7 was released in the fall of 2011, CogAT's Primary Battery (given to children in kindergarten through 2nd grade) added a brand new test area: Sentence Completion.

What exactly is the purpose of sentence completion in CogAT then? In the same paper, Dr. Lohman continued, "Good inferences both honor the syntactic constraints in the sentence and make full use of the conceptual information in it." In plain English, it means that: a. the grammar is correct; b. the sentence makes sense; and c. the sentence makes the most sense.

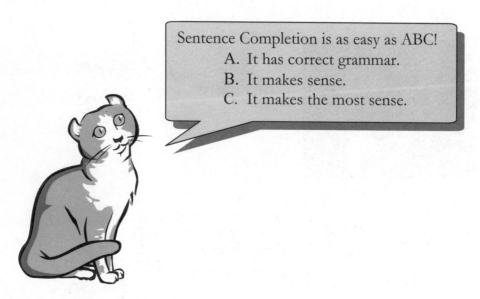

Sentence Completion is as easy as ABC!
A. It has correct grammar.
B. It makes sense.
C. It makes the most sense.

Let's see who is smarter, you or the Trapdog. First let's look at the example Dr. Lohman mentioned earlier.

1. Cats have two eyes but only one _____.

A. ears   B. ear   C. leg   D. paw   E. tail

First you rule out choices that are not correct from the grammar's point of view. Answer A is incorrect because *ears* is a plural noun and so *one ears* is not correct

English. The other four choices are all singular nouns. So the sentences based on these four choices are all valid English sentences.

Now you look at Answers B, C, and D. Normal cats do not have only one *ear*, or one *leg*, or one *paw*. It may be so for some very special cats, but that's not our everyday experience. **So Answer E. *tail* is the best answer**. Its grammar is correct; it makes sense; and it makes the most sense. Congratulations! You win the battle!

Now let's look at another example:

2. The fastest runner _____ the race.

J. loses   K. wins   L. watches   M. starts   N. makes

First you check the grammar. The sentence needs a third person verb. You check and see that all the answers are third person present tense verbs. So all five choices are correct from the grammar's point of view. Now you look at Answer J: *the fastest runner loses the race*. This does not happen very often and we need lots of explanation to understand why the fastest runner loses the race. So you rule out Answer J.

Answers L, M, and N are all valid. The fastest runner might *watch* the race, *start* the race, or *make* the race, but these choices do not make the most sense. **So finally you choose Answer K. *wins* because it is the best answer.** Congratulations! You win another battle!

What? You got the right answer? Now that little cat needs some fixing! I'll get you yet, "perfect scorer." Just wait... Verbal Classification is going to be fun! Ha ha ha!!

Chapter 5

Sentence Completion Practice Test

(20 questions, 10 minutes)

In the Sentence Completion subtest, students are given a sentence that is missing a word. Students must determine which of the available answers best completes the sentence.

1. The coach flipped a coin to _____ the tie.

A. even   B. break   C. make   D. join   E. bind

2. My dad _____ the train to work in the city.

J. drove   K. steered   L. flew   M. rode   N. road

3. Our ideas are similar; we think _____.

A. alike   B. together   C. out loud   D. creatively   E. out of the box

4. To my pleasant surprise, the faster I typed, the _____ mistakes I made.

J. less   K. least   L. more   M. most   N. fewer

5. Although she _____ homework, she knew that she had to do it.

A. loved   B. liked   C. disliked   D. enjoyed   E. cared about

6. I do not like overcooked steak, nor do I like it raw; I like it _____.

J. hot   K. cold   L. hard   M. soft   N. medium

7. Even though you use an avatar, you cannot really _____ your identity in the internet.

A. reveal   B. conceal   C. display   D. discover   E. tell

8. Matt and Nathan always _____ and disagree with each other.

J. play   K. work   L. agree   M. argue   N. corporate

9. Not only a bully at school, she is also _____ to animals.

A. bull   B. gentle   C. neutral   D. mean   E. carefree

10. Mary wears pink _____.

J. pajamas   K. jacket   L. shirt   M. scarf   N. dress

11. We bought some _____ in the coffee shop.

A. soaps   B. steaks   C. stamps   D. smoothies   E. vegetables

12. The principal's office is down the _____.

J. maze   K. mall   L. hall   M. ladder   N. tree

13. Hoping to _____ the conflict, they reached an agreement.

A. extend   B. start   C. increase   D. end   E. disagree

14. Jason _____ the door and locked it before he went to school.

J. opened   K. closed   L. bumped   M. kicked   N. blocked

15. _____ must use their library cards to check out videos and books from the public library of the city.

A. Mayor   B. Children   C. Students   D. Teachers   E. Patrons

16. Eric and I are neighbors; we live only three _____ away from each other.

J. streets   K. blocks   L. feet   M. houses   N. miles

17. May I _____ my ten-dollar bill with two of your five-dollar bills?

A. change   B. exchange   C. modify   D. alter   E. use

18. It took him a long time to decide, but at last James chose to play _____ in the school band.

J. Matterhorn   K. longhorn   L. game   M. saxophone   N. microphone

19. Although she _____ has time for her son, she plays with him whenever there is a chance.

A. never   B. always   C. sometimes   D. seldom   E. often

20. We have to elect a new mayor because our current one just submitted his _____.

J. report   K. budget   L. resignation   M. resume   N. application

Chapter 6

Sentence Completion Test Solutions

I recommend that you read through these solutions carefully even when you get the right answer. They might give you some insight into how to solve real CogAT problems.

1. In this question, a key phrase is *flipped a coin* which means *decided randomly*. The sentence tells us that there was a tie, and the coach decided to resolve it randomly. Answers A, C, D, and E are all incorrect because none of them resolved the tie. **So the best answer is B.** *break.*

2. First we see that the missing word must be a verb. So Answer N is ruled out. Second we notice that a train doesn't fly, so Answer L is not correct. Next we get clues from the context. The sentence says *to work in the city*, which means the train is just a commuting vehicle to go to the workplace. So *my dad* did not work on the train. Thus Answers J and K are ruled out. **So the best answer is M.** *rode.*

3. Let's look at the sentence structure. The two parts of the sentence are connected by a semicolon, which means that they are parallel. Now look at the first part of the sentence: *our ideas are similar*. The key word *similar* tells us that the best answer should be the one that matches it the best. Answers B, C, D, and E are all correct from the grammar's point of view, but their meanings are different from that of *similar*. **So the best answer is A.** *alike.*

4. Let's check grammar. Since *mistake* is a countable noun, we say *fewer* mistakes instead of *less* mistakes. So Answer J is ruled out. Notice that this question has a parallel structure: the faster …, the … So the right choice should be a comparison word like *faster*. Thus Answers K and M are ruled out. Now let's see which is better: *the faster I typed, the fewer mistakes I made;* or, *the faster I typed, the more mistakes I made.* From our common sense, the faster we type, the more likely we will make mistakes. However, it states at the be-

ginning of the sentence that it was *to my pleasant surprise*. This means the result is opposite to our common sense. **Therefore N. *fewer* is the correct answer.**

5. This sentence has the structure: *although ..., she knew that she had to do it.* It tells us that she was reluctant to do what she was supposed to do. Answers A, B, D, and E all indicate her willingness to do homework. They do not match the modifier *although*. **So the best answer is C. *disliked.***

6. This sentence states that overcooked steak is not desirable and raw steak is not desirable. **So the only correct choice is N. *medium.***

7. Let's look at the first part of the sentence: *even though you use an avatar.* People use avatar in the internet as a cover. The modifier *even though* indicates that such a cover does not really work. So the right answer should be a verb with a similar meaning as that of the verb *cover*. Thus Answers A, C, D, and E are not correct. **So the best answer is B. *conceal.***

8. The keyword here is *disagree*. It indicates that Matt and Nathan do not get along with each other. The right answer should honor this context clue. All answer choices are correct from the grammar's point of view. But Answers J, K, L, and N are not consistent with *disagree*. **Therefore the best answer is M. *argue.***

9. First we see that the word must be an adjective. So Answer A is ruled out. Next let's look at the structure of this sentence: not only ..., she is also ... It indicates that the two parallel parts are consistent with each other. Consistent behavior both inside and outside school indicates that she is also a bully to animals. So Answers B, C, and E are incorrect. **Therefore the best answer is D. *mean.***

10. Let's check grammar. Answers K, L, M, and N are all singular nouns. To make the sentence correct, we must say a pink *jacket*, a pink *shirt*, a pink *scarf*, or a pink *dress*. So none of them is correct. **Therefore the correct answer is J. *pajamas.***

11. The key phrase here is *the coffee shop*. Among the five choices, which one is the most likely item we might buy in a coffee shop? Answers A, B, C, and E are ruled out because they are not the most likely items you might buy in a coffee shop. **So the best answer is D. *smoothies.***

12. Here we get our context clue from the phrase *the principal's office*. Our common sense tells us that the principal's office should be somewhere inside the school building. So Answers J, K, M, and N do not make too much sense. **The best answer is L. *hall*.**

13. First we rule out Answer E because *hoping to disagree the conflict* does not make too much sense. Next we notice that *conflict* and *agreement* have opposite meanings. To reach an agreement must mean to resolve the conflict. Answers A, B, and C are not correct because instead of resolving the conflict, they make it worse. **So the best answer is D. *end*.**

14. Here the keyword is *locked*. What did Jason do to the door before he locked it? Answers L, M, and N were not logical things to do although they could happen. Answer J could happen, but it would not be the last step before locking the door. **Therefore the only answer left, K. *closed*, is the best answer.**

15. First we notice that the correct answer should be a plural noun. So Answer A is ruled out. Next we examine the key phrase *the public library of the city*. It tells us that although Answers B, C, and D are all valid, they are not the best because it is the city library, not the school library. **Therefore the best answer is E. *Patrons*.**

16. Here the keyword is *neighbors*. To be neighbors, Eric and I cannot live too far away from each other. So Answers J, K, and N are ruled out. Now look at Answer L. *feet*. It's not very common for neighbors to live only three feet away from each other. So Answer L is ruled out also. **Therefore the best answer is M. *houses*.**

17. Examining the sentence, we notice the fact that one ten-dollar bill has the same monetary value as two five-dollar bills. So it is a dollar for dollar exchange. Consequently Answers A, C, D, and E are ruled out because they are not the best answers. **Therefore the only answer left, B. *exchange*, is the right answer.**

18. The keyword here is *band*. So what James chose to play is a musical instrument. So Answers L and N are ruled out. Answer J is ruled out because it is the name of a location. Answer K is ruled out because it is the name of an animal. **So the right answer is M. *saxophone*.**

19. Let's look at the structure of the sentence: *although ..., she plays with him whenever there is a chance*. It indicates that she does not have a lot of time to spend with her son. So Answers B and E are ruled out. Answer A is incorrect because if she never had time, she would not be able to play with him at all. Finally we need to choose between Answer C. *sometimes* and Answer D. *seldom*. We see *seldom* is a better choice because it matches the context clue that she does not have a lot of time to spend with her son. **So D. *seldom* is the right answer.**

20. Here the key phrase is *elect a new mayor*. In light of this context clue, we see that Answers J, K, M, and N do not make the most sense because they fail to explain why we need to elect a new mayor. **Therefore the right answer is L. *resignation*.**

Chapter 7

Verbal Classification Traps and Tips

In the same paper "Beliefs about Ability and Accomplishment," Dr. Lohman wrote, "For measuring reasoning, the critical factor is not students' knowledge of infrequent words but rather the precision of their understandings of relatively common, but abstract words. Knowledge of infrequent or specialized words is actually a better measure of interest and specific achievement. Having only a vague understanding of the connotations of commonly used words is one of the oldest and most commonly observed characteristics of less able students."

Please read the last quoted sentence again and let it sink in. In Verbal Classification, nothing makes the Trapdog happier than seeing you confuse members of a group with the group itself.

> Mix up the category with the item!
> Mix up the category with the item!!
> Do it! Do it!! That's the best
> because then you'll fail! Ha ha ha!!!

Let's look at the following example.

1. apple   **orange**   **pear**

A. fruit   B. carrot   C. pea   D. lemon   E. onion

Here we see that all these three items are fruits. Please resist the temptation to choose the first answer choice *fruit*. This is exactly the trap set up by the Trapdog. While it's true that they are all fruits, they are actually members of the fruit family. Put it in another way, *fruit* has a higher order than that of *apple*, *orange*, or *pear*. When you classify them, remember to never mix up the orders. So Answer A is incorrect. Answers B, C, and E are not correct because they are all vegetables.

So the best answer is D. *lemon*.

Watch out! The Trapdog likes to confuse you with words that have multiple meanings. Be sure to think about all the meanings of a word before you choose an answer!

Another favorite trick of the Trapdog is using words that have more than one meaning. Let's look at the following example.

2. fire   **stove**   **iron**

J. wood   K. sink   L. match   M. rock   N. sun

This classification problem would be hard for you if you consider iron only as a plain metal. Don't be discouraged when you get stuck. Sit back, relax, and think if the words might have different meanings. Then you remember that iron also means an appliance used to press wrinkles from fabric when heated. Now you realize that *fire*, *stove*, and *iron* are all hot.

So you choose the right answer N. *sun*.

Drat! That cat slipped out of my claws! He has been telling you all my secrets!! GRRRRRR!! I'm MAD!! Just you wait, Number Analogies is next. I'll get you there! Mwua ha ha ha HA!!

Chapter 8

Verbal Classification Practice Test

(20 questions, 10 minutes)

In the Verbal Classification subtest, each question has two rows of words. In the top row, the student is given a set of three words that are similar in some way. Students must determine how they are similar and then select the word from the available answers that is most similar to the words in the top row.

1. square   rhombus   circle

A. shape   B. sphere   C. pyramid   D. cylinder   E. octagon

2. bark   burlap   sandpaper

J. silk   K. pinecone   L. paper   M. dog   N. burp

3. messy   sloppy   careless

A. tardy   B. untidy   C. late   D. sluggish   E. absent

4. lemon   orange   lime

J. apple   K. pear   L. banana   M. grape   N. grapefruit

5. twist   turn   bend

A. string   B. path   C. willow   D. wind   E. tornado

6. peninsula   island   cape

J. bay   K. isthmus   L. harbor   M. marina   N. inlet

7. after   since   till

A. time   B. behind   C. before   D. never   E. among

8. cork   feather   leaf

J. plug   K. ink   L. leather   M. brick   N. boat

9. defendant   prosecutor   judge

A. trial   B. jail   C. prisoner   D. witness   E. court

10. rose   porcupine   artichoke

J. tulip   K. hamster   L. cabbage   M. cactus   N. apple

11. gallon   pint   quart

A. cup   B. pound   C. meter   D. liter   E. gram

12. sunflower   dandelion   mustard

J. lavender   K. blueberry   L. broccoli   M. rose   N. banana

13. sunshine   sandwich   sleep

A. hot   B. burger   C. doze   D. spring   E. night

14. his   her   my

J. him   K. them   L. mine   M. us   N. our

15. sieve   spatula   fork

A. wrench   B. pliers   C. tongs   D. hammer   E. tool

16. season   month   second

J. day   K. watch   L. time   M. date   N. calendar

17. beside   against   along

A. under   B. over   C. attempt   D. near   E. upon

18. snake   lizard   alligator

J. eel   K. turtle   L. reptile   M. shark   N. frog

19. raft   tire   balloon

A. canoe   B. truck   C. beach ball   D. wagon   E. circle

20. cobweb   fishnet   basket

J. spider   K. fish   L. lace   M. basketball   N. internet

STOP

Chapter 9

Verbal Classification Test Solutions

I recommend that you read through these solutions carefully even when you get the right answer. They might give you some insight into how to solve real CogAT problems.

1. Examining the words in the top row, we see that they are all shapes. Answer A is ruled out because they are all members of the *shape* group and so do not have the same order as *shape*. Examining the words further, we see that *square*, *rhombus*, and *circle* are all two-dimensional shapes. So Answers B, C, and D are ruled out because they are three-dimensional shapes. **So the right answer is E. *octagon*.**

2. First we notice that *bark* has two meanings. One is a verb describing the sound of a dog. Another is a noun which means the outside of a tree trunk. Since *burlap* and *sandpaper* are both solid objects, the second meaning of *bark* makes sense here. Next we notice that what *bark*, *burlap*, and *sandpaper* have in common is that they are all rough. Answers J, L, and M are ruled out because they are not rough. Answer N is ruled out because *burp* is not a solid object. **So the best answer is K. *pinecone*.**

3. Inspecting these three words, we notice that they are all adjectives. Our five answer choices are also all adjectives. So nothing can be ruled out so far. Next we see that *absent* has nothing to do with *messy*, *sloppy*, or *careless*, so Answer E is ruled out. We also notice that *tardy* and *late* do not necessarily mean *messy*, so Answers A and C are ruled out. The same argument goes for *sluggish* because *sluggish* does not necessarily mean *messy*. Therefore Answer D is ruled out. **So the best answer is B. *untidy*.**

4. Looking at these three words, we notice that these three items are all fruits. Unfortunately our five answer choices are all members of the fruit family, so we cannot rule out any so far. Taking a close look at these three items *lemon*, *orange*, and *lime*, we see that they all belong to a special fruit family called citrus fruits. Now we can rule out Answers J, K, L, and M because they are not in the citrus fruit family. **The best answer is N. *grapefruit*.**

5. At first glance, we might not be able to spot anything in common between the top row words and any word in the second row. Looking closely, we notice that *wind* has two meanings. Its verb form means *twist* and *bend*. So Answers A, B, C, and E are all ruled out. **The only answer left, D. *wind*, is the best answer.**

6. These three items are all natural land formations. Answers J and N are ruled out because both of them represent body of water, not land formations. Answers L and M are ruled out because they are not natural land formations. **So the best answer is K. *isthmus*.**

7. To answer this question correctly, you might want to make a sentence so that all the three words in the top row can fit in more or less. For example, you can say: *after finishing my homework, I go out to play*. Or, *since I have finished my homework, I can go out to play*. Or, *I don't go out to play till I finish my homework*. Now you put the five choices into the sentence. You find that Answers A, B, and E do not work. So they are all ruled out. Answer C fits the sentence because we can say: *before finishing my homework, I cannot go out to play*. Answer D also fits the sentence because we can say: *I never go out to play because I need to finish my homework*. Now let's see which is better: *before* or *never*. We notice that none of the top row words is negative. **So Answer C. *before* is the best answer.**

8. Examining the three items in the top row, we notice that all of them are afloat. So Answers J, K, L, and M are not correct because none of them is afloat. **The best answer is N. *boat*.**

9. Each of these three words means a person. So Answers A, B, and E are ruled out because none of them means a person. We also notice that all the words in the top row are related to a court. So Answer C. *prisoner* is ruled out because a prisoner does not usually appear in a court. **So the best answer is D. *witness*.**

10. We notice that each of these three words means something that has spikes. So Answers J, K, L, and N are ruled out because none of them has spikes. **So the best answer is M. *cactus*.**

11. Inspecting the three words in the top row, we notice that they are all measurements of volume. So Answers B, C, and E are ruled out. Next we notice that all these three measurements are in the customary system, so Answer D

is ruled out because *liter* is in the metric system. **Therefore the best answer is A. *cup*.**

12. Looking at the three items in the top row, we notice that they all have yellow color. So Answers J, K, L, and M are ruled out because none of them is yellow. **The best answer is N. *banana*.**

13. We examine the three words and find that they do not have a lot in common other than the fact that they all start with the letter *s*. **So the best answer is D. *spring*.** Please remember that if the three words have other common characteristics, then we should consider these other common characteristics first and find a word that matches these common characteristics. Words with the same letter to start with should not be our primary concern.

14. For a group like this, making up a phrase might be a good way to help us choose the right answer. We can say *his book*, *her book*, or *my book*. Now we look at the five answer choices and find that Answers J, K, L, and M don't fit our phrase. **So the best answer is N. *our*.**

15. First we see that the three items in the top row are all tools. Answer E is ruled out because *tool* is a general term and therefore has a higher order than that of a *sieve*, a *spatula*, or a *fork*. Looking at these three items more closely, we notice that they are all related to cooking and eating. So Answers A, B, and D are all ruled out because they are not commonly associated with food. **Therefore Answer C. *tongs* is the right answer.**

16. These three words are all measurements of time. Answer L is ruled out because *time* is a general term and therefore has a higher order than that of individual measurements of time. Answers K and N are ruled out because although we use *watch* and *calendar* to keep track of time, *watch* and *calendar* are not measurements of time. Answer M is ruled out because a *date* is a particular moment of time instead of a measurement of time. **So the best answer is J. *day*.**

17. Examining these three words and we find that they are all prepositions. Answer C is ruled out because *attempt* is a verb. Looking at them closely, we find that *beside*, *against*, and *along* all mean close to something. So Answers A, B, and E are ruled out. **Therefore the only answer left, D. *near*, is the best answer.**

18. These three animals are all reptiles. Answer L is ruled out because *reptile* is a general term and therefore has a higher order than that of the members of the reptile family. Answer M is ruled out because a *shark* is a fish, not a reptile. Answer J is ruled out because although it looks like a snake, *eel* is actually a fish. Answer N is ruled out because a *frog* is an amphibian, not a reptile. **So the best answer is K. *turtle*.**

19. At first glance, we might want to choose Answer A. *canoe* because it is similar to raft. But it does not work because unlike *raft*, *canoe*, and *balloon*, a *tire* does not float. So Answer A is ruled out. Examining the three words in the top row further, we notice that one of the meanings of *raft* is an inflatable craft for floating on water. Now we see that *raft*, *tire*, and *balloon* have one thing in common: they are all inflated. So Answers B, D, and E are ruled out because they are not inflated. **So Answer C. *beach ball* is the right choice.**

20. Inspecting the three words in the top row, we notice that they are all kind of like nets. So Answers J, K, and M are ruled out. Answer N is ruled out because an *internet* is not a touchable net like the items in the top row. **So the best answer is L. *lace*.**

Part Two

Quantitative

Chapter 10

Number Analogies Traps and Tips

There are some common myths surrounding the CogAT. One is that it's unethical to prepare for it. However, for CogAT Form 7, Riverside Publishing developed its own teacher guides and student practice booklets to help teach thinking skills. You have to ask why the test publisher would do so if it is "unethical."

Another common myth is that an ability test is not something you can prepare for. I can think of two groups of people in this camp. In the first group are the test designers. For these people, the more mysterious the test is, the better it would serve their self interest. In the second group are those who think that either you have the ability or you don't. Those people tend to think that either I am smart or I am not. There is nothing I can do about it and I am not responsible for it. Indeed, it is unsettling to think that you can improve your abilities because that means you need to **work** to reach your potential. Work is not something very attractive in our consumer oriented society in which delayed gratification is not valued. However, the fact that you have read this book thus far means that you do not belong to this group and therefore do not buy this line of thinking.

In CogAT <u>Report to Parents</u>, Riverside states that "CogAT measures learned reasoning and problem-solving skills." If it is "learned," then we can learn it, and this book is a great place to learn it. Now let's learn how to solve CogAT number analogies problems. Like verbal analogies, we need to make a bridge sentence that is valid for both pairs in number analogies questions. Remember to always try addition, subtraction, multiplication, or division first when making a bridge sentence because these four operations represent the majority of the questions in number analogies.

> Tip: For number analogies, first try to make a bridge sentence using addition, subtraction, multiplication, or division. If that doesn't work, you can try squares, prime numbers, or Fibonacci numbers.

Let's see if you can outsmart the Trapdog. Look at this example:

1. [2 → 5]   [4 → 9]   [3 → ?]

A. 4   B. 5   C. 6   D. 7   E. 8

First let's try a bridge sentence like this: 5 is three more than 2. This bridge doesn't work because 9 is not three more than 4. As in verbal analogies, don't be discouraged if your initial bridge does not hold the weight. Looking at the pairs carefully, you notice that 5 is one plus the double of 2. To see if this bridge works, you need to test if 9 is one plus the double of 4. It is!

So now you know how to solve this analogy. The right answer should be one plus the double of 3, which is 7. **So Answer D. 7 is the right answer.**

Now let's look at another example.

2. [17 → 5]   [23 → 11]   [30 → ?]

J. 13   K. 15   L. 18   M. 20   N. 22

First you might want to test if the following bridge sentence works: 17 minus twelve is 5. Now is 23 minus twelve 11? It is. Your bridge works! **So the right answer is 30 minus twelve, which is L. 18.** Congratulations! You win another round!

Hmmm… I think I know what I'm doing wrong! That little cat always finds my trap and tells you before you fall for it. GRRRRR! I'll get you on Number Puzzles! They're my favorite!

Chapter 11

Number Analogies Practice Test

(18 questions, 10 minutes)

In the Number Analogies subtest, students are given two pairs of numbers and another number without its pair. The first two pairs of numbers are related in some way. Students must determine how they are related and then select the number from the available answers that has the same relationship with the number in the third pair.

1. [1 → 2]   [2 → 4]   [5 → ?]

A. 4   B. 10   C. 8   D. 12   E. 6

2. [4 → 3]   [5 → 4]   [7 → ?]

J. 7   K. 5   L. 6   M. 4   N. 8

3. [4 → 9]   [16 → 25]   [36 → ?]

A. 121   B. 225   C. 63   D. 49   E. 91

4. [54 → 27]   [76 → 38]   [34 → ?]

J. 21   K. 17   L. 18   M. 30   N. 13

5. **[3 → 9]**   **[4 → 16]**   **[13 → ?]**

A. 169   B. 225   C. 121   D. 256   E. 196

6. **[9 → 3]**   **[15 → 5]**   **[81 → ?]**

J. 27   K. 9   L. 15   M. 11   N. 21

7. **[2 → 3]**   **[5 → 7]**   **[19 → ?]**

A. 20   B. 21   C. 22   D. 23   E. 24

8. **[20 → 9]**   **[30 → 14]**   **[40 → ?]**

J. 16   K. 15   L. 18   M. 17   N. 19

9. **[7 → 21]**   **[5 → 19]**   **[2 → ?]**

A. 15   B. 14   C. 13   D. 16   E. 17

10. **[17 → 14]**   **[21 → 18]**   **[32 → ?]**

J. 31   K. 29   L. 30   M. 28   N. 32

11. **[4 → 8]**   **[16 → 32]**   **[37 → ?]**

A. 72   B. 70   C. 74   D. 78   E. 64

12. **[2 → 8]**   **[3 → 27]**   **[4 → ?]**

J. 32   K. 128   L. 64   M. 16   N. 256

13. [8 → 2]   [13 → 7]   [21 → ?]

A. 15   B. 14   C. 13   D. 16   E. 17

14. [36 → 6]   [100 → 10]   [144 → ?]

J. 12   K. 16   L. 20   M. 18   N. 14

15. [128 → 32]   [96 → 24]   [32 → ?]

A. 16   B. 4   C. 6   D. 8   E. 2

16. [3 → 0]   [5 → 0]   [9 → ?]

J. 0   K. 4   L. 2   M. 3   N. 1

17. [10 → 40]   [30 → 120]   [40 → ?]

A. 240   B. 160   C. 220   D. 200   E. 180

18. [21 → 4]   [34 → 17]   [53 → ?]

J. 39   K. 36   L. 38   M. 37   N. 35

STOP

Chapter 12

Number Analogies Test Solutions

I recommend that you read through these solutions carefully even when you get the right answer. They might give you some insight into how to solve real CogAT problems.

1. First let's find the positive difference between the first and the second number in each pair. Since the positive difference between 1 and 2 is 1, and the positive difference between 2 and 4 is 2, we do not find a bridge here. Next let's try ratios. The ratio of 2 over 1 is 2; the ratio of 4 over 2 is 2. So this bridge works! **So the right answer is 2 times 5, which is B. 10.**

2. Let's find the positive difference between the first and the second number in each pair again. Since the positive difference between 4 and 3 is 1, and the positive difference between 5 and 4 is 1, this bridge works. **So the right answer is 7 minus 1, which is L. 6.**

3. As always, let's try the positive difference between the first and the second number in each pair. Since the positive difference between 4 and 9 is 5, and the positive difference between 16 and 25 is 9, this bridge does not work. Next let's try ratios. We find that neither 9/4 nor 4/9 is an integer. So this bridge does not work either. Finally we notice that 4 is the square of 2; 9 is the square of 3; and the difference between 2 and 3 is 1. To see if this bridge holds the weight, we need to check if 16 is the square of a number, and if 25 is the square of another number, and furthermore if the difference between these two numbers is 1. We see that 16 is the square of 4; 25 is the square of 5; and the difference between 4 and 5 is 1. So this bridge works! So now to solve this problem, first we need to find a number such that its square is 36. We find that the square of 6 is 36. Next we add 1 to 6 and get the number 7. **Finally, the right answer should be the square of 7, which is D. 49.**

4. As a first try, let's find the positive difference between the first and the second number in each pair. The positive difference between 54 and 27 is 27;

and that between 76 and 38 is 38. Since this positive difference is not a constant, let's try ratios. The ratio of 54 over 27 is 2. The ratio of 76 over 38 is 2. So this bridge works. **So the right answer is 34 over 2 which is K. 17.**

5. As before, let's find the positive difference between the first and the second number in each pair. Since the positive difference between 3 and 9 is 6, and that between 4 and 16 is 12, this bridge does not work. Next let's try ratios. Since the ratio of 9 over 3 is 3, and the ratio of 16 over 4 is 4, this bridge does not work either. Finally we notice that 9 is the square of 3. To see if this bridge works, we need to check if 16 is the square of 4. It is. So the right answer should be the square of 13, which is 169. **So the right answer is A. 169.**

6. We check the positive difference between the first and the second number in each pair first. Since 9 minus 3 is 6, and 15 minus 5 is 10, this bridge does not work. Next let's check ratios. Since 9 over 3 is 3 and 15 over 5 is 3, this bridge works. So the right answer is 81 over 3. **So the right answer is J. 27.**

7. Let's give it a try to find the positive difference between the first and the second number in each pair. Since the positive difference between 2 and 3 is 1, and that between 5 and 7 is 2, this bridge does not work. Next we check ratios and find that neither 3/2 nor 2/3 is an integer. Next let's see if one number might be the square of another number in each pair, and the answer again is a "no." Then we notice that 2 and 3 are consecutive prime numbers. Also 5 and 7 are consecutive prime numbers. So we find a bridge at last! The correct answer should be the next prime number after 19. **So the right answer is D. 23.**

8. As a first step, let's find the positive difference between the first and the second number in each pair. Since the positive difference between 20 and 9 is 11, and that between 30 and 14 is 16, this bridge does not work. Next let's try ratios. We see that neither 20/9 nor 9/20 is an integer. Then we notice that 9 is one half of 20 minus one. To see if this bridge works, we need to check if one half of 30 minus one is 14. It is! So this bridge works. The right answer should be one half of 40 minus 1, which is 19. **So the right answer is N. 19.**

9. Difference is always the first thing we check. We see that the positive difference between 7 and 21 is 14. The positive difference between 5 and 19 is 14. So this bridge works. The right answer should be 2 plus 14. **So the right answer is D. 16.**

10. Many times the simplest thing is the best thing as well. Let's find the positive difference between the first and the second number in each pair. Since the positive difference between 17 and 14 is three, and the positive difference between 21 and 18 is three, this bridge works. So the right answer is 32 minus three. **So the right answer is K. 29.**

11. First let us find the positive difference between the first and the second number in each pair. Since the positive difference between 4 and 8 is 4, and the positive difference between 16 and 32 is 16, this bridge does not work. Next let's try ratios. Since 8 over 4 is two, and 32 over 16 is two, this bridge holds the weight. So the right answer is two times 37. **Therefore the right answer is C. 74.**

12. As always, let's find the positive difference between the first and the second number in each pair. Since the positive difference between 2 and 8 is 6, and the positive difference between 3 and 27 is 24, this bridge does not work. Next let's try ratios. We see that 8 over 2 is 4, which is the square of 2. We also see that 27 over 3 is 9, which is the square of 3. So the right answer should be 4 times the square of 4. **Therefore the right answer is L. 64.**

13. First thing first, let's find the positive difference between the first and the second number in each pair. Since the positive difference between 8 and 2 is 6, and the positive difference between 13 and 7 is 6, this bridge works. So the right answer is 21 minus 6. **So the right answer is A. 15.**

14. As before, let's find the positive difference between the first and the second number in each pair. Since the positive difference between 36 and 6 is 30, and the positive difference between 100 and 10 is 90, this bridge does not work. Next let's check ratios. Since 36 over 6 is 6, and 100 over 10 is 10, this bridge does not work either. Examining the pairs further, we notice that 36 is the square of 6 and 100 is the square of 10. So the right answer should be some number such that its square is 144. **So the right answer is J. 12 because the square of 12 is 144.**

15. As a first step, let's find the positive difference between the first and the second number in each pair. Since 128 minus 32 is 96 and 96 minus 24 is 72, this bridge does not work. Next let's check ratios. 128 over 32 is 4; 96 over 24 is also 4. So this bridge works. So the right answer is 32 over 4. **So the right answer is D. 8.**

16. Let's give it a try to find the positive difference between the first and the second number in each pair. Since the positive difference between 3 and 0 is 3, and the positive difference between 5 and 0 is 5, this bridge does not work. Next let's check ratios. 0 over 3 is zero. 0 over 5 is zero. So this bridge holds the weight. The right answer is 9 times zero. **So the right answer is J. 0.**

17. First let's find the positive difference between the first and the second number in each pair. Since the positive difference between 10 and 40 is 30, and the positive difference between 30 and 120 is 90, this bridge does not work. Next let's check ratios. 40 over 10 is four. 120 over 30 is four. So this bridge works. So the right answer is 40 times four. **So the right answer is B. 160.**

18. Difference is always the first thing we check. Since the positive difference between 21 and 4 is 17, and that between 34 and 17 is 17, this bridge works. So the right answer is 53 minus 17. **So the right answer is K. 36.**

Chapter 13

Number Puzzles Traps and Tips

Ha ha! These quantitative sections are my specialty, especially number puzzles! You little failures don't even know basic algebra! My number puzzles'll get you for sure! Mwua ha ha ha ha!!

The number puzzles subtest has the fewest questions, 16 in total. Among all nine subtests, only number puzzles and paper folding have 16 questions each. What does it mean? It means that number puzzles and paper folding questions are the hardest of all CogAT subtests. There are two ways to solve number puzzles: one, replacing the question mark with each answer choice to check which is the right answer; and two, using a little algebra.

Let's use both methods to solve the following number puzzle.

1. $? = \blacksquare + 2$

    $\blacksquare = 4 - ?$

A. 0   B. 1   C. 2   D. 3   E. 4

In this type of question, we must substitute the value of ■ into the equation to determine the value of the question mark. So now we have:

$$? = 4 - ? + 2$$

Solution One: replacing the question mark with each answer choice until we find the right answer.

To see which answer choice is right, we place each of them into the equation and check until we find the right one. We see that $0 \neq 4 - 0 + 2$; $1 \neq 4 - 1 + 2$; $2 \neq 4 - 2 + 2$; but $3 = 4 - 3 + 2$. **So the right answer is D. 3.**

Solution Two: using algebra.

The equation is: $? = 4 - ? + 2$. To solve it, we add ? to both the left and the right side of the equation. The equation will still hold because we add the same amount to both sides. So now we have: $? + ? = ? + 4 - ? + 2$. Since $? - ? = 0$, we have $? + ? = 4 + 0 + 2$. So we have $? + ? = 6$. Now we see $? = 3$. **So the right answer is D. 3.**

Next let's look at another example.

2. $\dfrac{56}{?} > 7$

J. 6   K. 8   L. 10   M. 12   N. 24

Tip: Watch out for the sign. Do not mistake the ">" or "<" sign for an "=" sign. If two positive fractions have a common numerator, then the larger the denominator, the smaller the fraction.

For this type of question, remember that if two positive fractions have a common numerator, then the larger the denominator, the smaller the fraction. Since $7 \times 8 = 56$, we have that:

$$\frac{56}{?} < 7 \text{ if } ? > 8,$$

$$\frac{56}{?} = 7 \text{ if } ? = 8, \text{ and}$$

$$\frac{56}{?} > 7 \text{ if } ? < 8.$$

Therefore the right answer must be less than eight. We see that only answer choice J is less than eight. **So the right answer is J. 6.**

Chapter 14

Number Puzzles Practice Test

(16 questions, 10 minutes)

In the Number Puzzles subtest, students are given a mathematical equation and students must determine the number from the available answers that should replace the question mark in the equation.

1. $4 - ? = 1$

A. 4   B. 3   C. 2   D. 1   E. 0

2. $5 \times 3 \times ? = 75$

J. 1   K. 3   L. 5   M. 7   N. 9

3. $8 + ? + 2 + \square = 23$

$\square = 10$

A. 0   B. 1   C. 2   D. 3   E. 4

4. $\dfrac{70}{?} + 26 = 36$

J. 4   K. 5   L. 6   M. 7   N. 8

5. $(8 + 4) \times 2 = ? \times 6$

A. 0   B. 1   C. 2   D. 3   E. 4

6. $\square + \blacktriangle = ? + 2$

     $\square = 5$

     $\blacktriangle = \square - 2$

J. 4   K. 6   L. 8   M. 10   N. 12

7. $\dfrac{63}{?} = 9$

A. 5   B. 6   C. 7   D. 8   E. 9

8. $(3 \times 7) \times 6 = 6 \times (7 \times ?)$

J. 1   K. 3   L. 5   M. 7   N. 9

9. $\dfrac{36}{?} < 3$

A. 9   B. 10   C. 11   D. 12   E. 13

10. $5 - 1 + 6 - 1 > ? + 2$

J. 6   K. 7   L. 8   M. 9   N. 10

11. $10 - \blacktriangle = ? + \blacksquare$

      $\blacktriangle = ?$

      $\blacksquare = 4 - ?$

A. 4   B. 5   C. 6   D. 7   E. 8

12. $\dfrac{72}{?} > 9$

J. 6   K. 8   L. 9   M. 12   N. 27

13. $(7 + 9) + 5 < (? + 5) + 9$

A. 4   B. 5   C. 6   D. 7   E. 8

14. $\dfrac{?}{8} > 6$

J. 20   K. 24   L. 32   M. 48   N. 54

15. $(12 - 5 + 3) / 2 = ? + 3 - 1$

A. 0   B. 1   C. 2   D. 3   E. 4

16. $10 - \blacktriangledown > ? - 2$

      $\blacktriangledown = 5$

J. 6   K. 7   L. 8   M. 9   N. 1

Chapter 15

Number Puzzles Test Solutions

I recommend that you read through these solutions carefully even when you get the right answer. They might give you some insight into how to solve real CogAT problems.

1. In this question, we need to find out which answer choice can replace the question mark so as to make the equation hold true. We subtract one to both sides of the equation $4 - ? = 1$ and get $4 - 1 - ? = 1 - 1$. So $3 - ? = 0$. Therefore $? = 3$. **So the right answer is B. 3.**

2. For this question, let's put each answer choice into the equation to see if the equation holds or not. We see that $5 \times 3 \times 1 \neq 75$; $5 \times 3 \times 3 \neq 75$; but $5 \times 3 \times 5 = 75$. **So the right answer is L. 5.**

3. First we replace □ with 10, and get the equation we need to solve: $8 + ? + 2 + 10 = 23$. Next let's put each answer choice into the equation to see which one holds. We see that $8 + 0 + 2 + 10 \neq 23$; $8 + 1 + 2 + 10 \neq 23$; $8 + 2 + 2 + 10 \neq 23$; but $8 + 3 + 2 + 10 = 23$. **So the right answer is D. 3.**

4. To make the equation valid, the number to replace the question mark must be a factor of 70. Of the five answer choices, only Answers K and M are factors of 70. So Answers J, L, and N are ruled out. We see that $70 / 5 + 26 \neq 36$, but $70 / 7 + 26 = 36$. **So the right answer is M. 7.**

5. Let's use algebra to solve this problem. Since $(8 + 4) \times 2 = 24$, we can re-write the equation as $24 = ? \times 6$. Since $4 \times 6 = 24$, we have that $? = 4$. **So the right answer is E. 4.**

6. First we replace □ and ▲ with their values. Since □ $= 5$ and ▲ $=$ □ $- 2$, we have that ▲ $= 5 - 2 = 3$. Placing both values into the equation, we get $5 + 3 = ? + 2$. Next let's replace the question mark with answer choices to see which one is right. We see that $5 + 3 \neq 4 + 2$, but $5 + 3 = 6 + 2$. **So the right answer is K. 6.**

7. The answer choice to replace the question mark must be a factor of 63 to hold the equation. Since A, B, and D are not factors of 63, they are ruled out. Answer E is ruled out because 63 / 9 ≠ 9. **So the right answer is C. 7.**

8. Let's replace the question mark with each answer choice to see which one holds. We see that $(3 \times 7) \times 6 \neq 6 \times (7 \times 1)$, but $(3 \times 7) \times 6 = 6 \times (7 \times 3)$. **So the right answer is K. 3.**

9. To solve this inequality, first let's see which value "x" makes the equation 36 / x = 3 true. We see that when x = 12, 36 / 12 = 3. So Answer D. 12 is ruled out because 36/12 is equal to, not less than, three. We know that for two fractions with a common numerator, the smaller the denominator, the larger the fraction. So Answers A, B, and C are ruled out because 36 / ? > 3 when ? is replaced with any of these answer choices. **So the right answer is E. 13.**

10. We solve this inequality with algebra. Since 5 − 1 + 6 − 1 = 9, we rewrite the inequality as 9 > ? + 2. Now we subtract 2 from both sides of the inequality and get 9 − 2 > ? + 2 − 2. So 7 > ? + 0. So 7 > ? . Of all answer choices, only Answer J is less than 7. **So the right answer is J. 6.**

11. Again, we solve this problem with algebra. First we replace ▲ and ■ with their values in the equation and rewrite the equation as 10 − ? = ? + 4 − ?. Since ? − ? = 0, we have 10 − ? = 4. We subtract 4 from both sides and get 10 − 4 − ? = 4 − 4. So 6 − ? = 0. **So the right answer is C. 6.**

12. To solve this inequality, first let's solve the equation 72 / x = 9. We see that when x = 8, 72 / x = 9. We know that for two fractions with a common numerator, the smaller the denominator, the larger the fraction. So the value of the question mark must be less than 8 so as to make 72 / ? > 9. **So the right answer is J. 6.**

13. Let's solve this inequality with algebra. First let's subtract 5 from both sides. We have (7 + 9) + 5 − 5 < (? + 5) + 9 − 5. So 7 + 9 < ? + 9. Next we subtract 9 from both sides and get 7 + 9 − 9 < ? + 9 − 9. So 7 < ?. **So the right answer is E. 8.**

14. To solve this inequality, first let's solve the equation x / 8 = 6. We see that when x = 48, x / 8 = 6. Now to make ? / 8 > 6 true, the value of the question mark must be greater than 48. **So the right answer is N. 54.**

15. Let's solve the equation with algebra. Since $(12 - 5 + 3) / 2 = 5$, we rewrite the equation as $5 = ? + 3 - 1$. So $5 = ? + 2$. Next we subtract 2 from both sides of the equation and get: $5 - 2 = ? + 2 - 2$. So $3 = ? + 0$. So $3 = ?$. **So the right answer is D. 3.**

16. First let's replace ▼ with its value 5 in the inequality and get $10 - 5 > ? - 2$. Next we replace the question mark with each answer choice to check which holds the inequality. Since $10 - 5 > 6 - 2$, **the right answer is J. 6.**

Chapter 16

Number Series Traps and Tips

Before we move on to number series, let's review what CogAT test designers think we are capable of in the area of quantitative reasoning, shall we? According to Case and Okamoto,* children from age 5 to 11 are at the *dimensional* stage, which is comprised of several levels.

1. A typical four-year old thinks at the *pre-dimensional* level. He can answer questions such as "Which of these two piles of chips has more?" He compares two piles of chips and tells us which pile has more.

2. A typical six-year old thinks at the *unidimensional* level. She can answer questions such as "Which is more, 5, or 4?" She makes a mental number line, counts 5, then counts 4, and tells us which is more.

3. A typical eight-year old thinks at the *bidimensional* level. He can answer questions such as "What is the largest two-digit number you can think of?" He can use two mental number lines, one for the tens digit, the other for the ones digit, and tell us the largest two-digit number.

4. A typical ten-year old thinks at the *integrated bidimensional* level. She can answer questions such as "Which difference is bigger, the difference between 7 and 9 or the difference between 2 and 5?" She creates one mental number line to find the difference between 7 and 9. She creates another mental number line to find the difference between 2 and 5. Then she tells us which difference is bigger.

You might want to ask what happens after age 10. According to Case, starting from eleven, kids begin to coordinate two or more dimensions into one abstract vector and enter into the *vectorial* stage. However, a person's number sense and therefore the ability to solve the Number Series problems in CogAT is well developed at age ten.

* Case, R., & Okamoto, Y. (1996). The role of central conceptual structures in the development of children's thought. *Monographs of the Society for Research in Child Development, 61* (1–2, Serial No. 246).

For Number Series problems, a good approach is to look at the gaps between consecutive numbers. The gap can be either the difference or the ratio between two consecutive numbers in the series. This helps us uncover the pattern of the series most of the time. The Trapdog loves to fool us by setting up uneven gaps. Many times children are fooled because after checking the first gap, we mistakenly think that this gap applies to all the numbers in the series. In order to solve number series problems correctly, it's important to check all the gaps and understand the pattern of the gaps. In case neither the difference nor the ratio works, we should check and see if the sum or the product of two consecutive numbers in the series might give us clues.

Now let's look at a number series example.

1.   1 2 4 5 7 8 →

A. 7   B. 8   C. 9   D. 10   E. 11

Ha ha!! A few bumpy gaps will really throw you for a ride! A ride to failure! Mwua ha ha ha!

The difference between the first two numbers in the series is 1. Do not leap into the conclusion that this is the gap between all the consecutive numbers in the series! Examining the series further, we see that the gaps have this pattern: +1, +2, +1, +2, +1. So the next gap should be +2. Therefore the right answer should be 8 + 2 = 10.

So Answer D. 10 is the right answer.

Tip: For number series problems, check all the gaps! Be sure to know exactly what the pattern is and whatever crazy rules it follows! Or else you'll fall right into the Trapdog's claws!

Now let's look at another example.

2.   2 4 6 2 4 →

J. 2   K. 3   L. 4   M. 5   N. 6

We see that the series repeats itself every three numbers. So the next number should be 6. **So Answer N. 6 is the right answer.**

Chapter 17

Number Series Practice Test

(18 questions, 10 minutes)

In the Number Series subtest, the student is shown a series of numbers. Students need to review the numbers to determine the rule or pattern used and then select the number from the answer choices that should come next in the series.

1.   4 7 2 4 7 →

A. 7   B. 4   C. 2   D. 10   E. 9

2.   20 5 19 4 18 →

J. 17   K. 3   L. 21   M. 6   N. 2

3.   12 6 24 12 48 →

A. 18   B. 96   C. 3   D. 24   E. 36

4.   3 6 10 15 21 →

J. 24   K. 25   L. 26   M. 27   N. 28

5.   10 9 9 8 8 →

A. 8   B. 9   C. 7   D. 10   E. 6

6.   5 8 13 20 29 →

J. 38   K. 40   L. 32   M. 36   N. 34

7.   90 75 77 62 64 →

A. 49   B. 64   C. 59   D. 60   E. 79

8.   16 4 1 $\dfrac{1}{4}$ $\dfrac{1}{16}$ →

J. $\dfrac{1}{32}$ K. $\dfrac{1}{64}$ L. $\dfrac{1}{128}$ M. 32   N. 64

9.   10 10 20 30 50 →

A. 100   B. 80   C. 60   D. 70   E. 90

10.   3 9 4 12 7 →

J. 12   K. 21   L. 2   M. 15   N. 13

11. $\dfrac{1}{2}$ $\dfrac{3}{4}$ $\dfrac{5}{8}$ $\dfrac{7}{16}$ $\dfrac{9}{32}$ →

A. $\dfrac{5}{32}$ B. $\dfrac{11}{32}$ C. $\dfrac{11}{64}$ D. $\dfrac{9}{64}$ E. $\dfrac{9}{128}$

12.   27 37 35 45 43 →

J. 41   K. 33   L. 45   M. 53   N. 55

13.   2 3 6 18 108 →

A. 1944   B. 648   C. 324   D. 1024   E. 216

14.   5 11 17 23 29 →

J. 31   K. 33   L. 35   M. 37   N. 39

15.   11 9 18 16 32 →

A. 64   B. 22   C. 30   D. 24   E. 48

16.   4 9 16 25 36 →

J. 48   K. 49   L. 50   M. 64   N. 27

17.   2 3 5 8 13 →

A. 14   B. 16   C. 21   D. 18   E. 15

18.   55 45 36 28 21 →

J. 20   K. 18   L. 15   M. 13   N. 11

Quantitative Battery Bubble Form

Number Analogies

1. (A) (B) (C) (D) (E)
2. (J) (K) (L) (M) (N)
3. (A) (B) (C) (D) (E)
4. (J) (K) (L) (M) (N)
5. (A) (B) (C) (D) (E)
6. (J) (K) (L) (M) (N)
7. (A) (B) (C) (D) (E)
8. (J) (K) (L) (M) (N)
9. (A) (B) (C) (D) (E)
10. (J) (K) (L) (M) (N)
11. (A) (B) (C) (D) (E)
12. (J) (K) (L) (M) (N)
13. (A) (B) (C) (D) (E)
14. (J) (K) (L) (M) (N)
15. (A) (B) (C) (D) (E)
16. (J) (K) (L) (M) (N)
17. (A) (B) (C) (D) (E)
18. (J) (K) (L) (M) (N)

Number Puzzles

1. (A) (B) (C) (D) (E)
2. (J) (K) (L) (M) (N)
3. (A) (B) (C) (D) (E)
4. (J) (K) (L) (M) (N)
5. (A) (B) (C) (D) (E)
6. (J) (K) (L) (M) (N)
7. (A) (B) (C) (D) (E)
8. (J) (K) (L) (M) (N)
9. (A) (B) (C) (D) (E)
10. (J) (K) (L) (M) (N)
11. (A) (B) (C) (D) (E)
12. (J) (K) (L) (M) (N)
13. (A) (B) (C) (D) (E)
14. (J) (K) (L) (M) (N)
15. (A) (B) (C) (D) (E)
16. (J) (K) (L) (M) (N)

Number Series

1. (A) (B) (C) (D) (E)
2. (J) (K) (L) (M) (N)
3. (A) (B) (C) (D) (E)
4. (J) (K) (L) (M) (N)
5. (A) (B) (C) (D) (E)
6. (J) (K) (L) (M) (N)
7. (A) (B) (C) (D) (E)
8. (J) (K) (L) (M) (N)
9. (A) (B) (C) (D) (E)
10. (J) (K) (L) (M) (N)
11. (A) (B) (C) (D) (E)
12. (J) (K) (L) (M) (N)
13. (A) (B) (C) (D) (E)
14. (J) (K) (L) (M) (N)
15. (A) (B) (C) (D) (E)
16. (J) (K) (L) (M) (N)
17. (A) (B) (C) (D) (E)
18. (J) (K) (L) (M) (N)

Chapter 18

Number Series Test Solutions

I recommend that you read through these solutions carefully even when you get the right answer. They might give you some insight into how to solve real CogAT problems.

1. In this problem, the numbers repeat themselves every three numbers. **So the right answer is C. 2.**

2. First let's find the differences between consecutive numbers to see if we can find the pattern of this series. We see the gaps are: −15, +14, −15, +14. To continue this pattern, the next gap must be −15. So the next number should be 18 − 15. **So the right answer is K. 3.**

3. As always, let's first find the differences between consecutive numbers to see if we can find the pattern of this series. We see that the gaps are: −6, +18, −12, +36. Since there is no pattern here, let's try ratios. This time we see: /2, ×4, /2, ×4. Now we see the pattern. So the next number should be 48 / 2 = 24. **Therefore the right answer is D. 24.**

4. As before, let's find the differences between consecutive numbers. We see the gaps are: +3, +4, +5, +6. So the next number should be 21 + 7. **So the right answer is N. 28.**

5. Difference is always the first thing we check. Let's find the differences between consecutive numbers. We see the gaps are: −1, +0, −1, +0. So the next number should be 8 − 1. **So the right answer is C. 7.**

6. First thing first, let's find the differences between consecutive numbers. We see the gaps are: +3, +5, +7, +9. So the next number should be 29 + 11. **So the right answer is K. 40.**

7. As a first try, let's find the differences between consecutive numbers. We see the gaps are: −15, +2, −15, +2. So the next number should be 64 − 15. **So the right answer is A. 49.**

8. Let's give it a try to find the differences between consecutive numbers. We see the gaps are: −12, −3, −3/4, −3/16. Since there is no pattern here, let's try ratios between consecutive numbers to see if we can find the pattern of the series this way. This time we see: /4, /4, /4, /4. So the next number should be (1/16)/4. **So the right answer is K. 1/64.**

9. As a first step, let's find the differences between consecutive numbers. We see the gaps are: +0, +10, +10, +20. Since there is no pattern here, let's try ratios between consecutive numbers to see if we can find the pattern of the series this way. Since neither 20/30 nor 30/20 is an integer, this doesn't work either. Furthermore, we do not see any patterns of prime numbers or squares. Finally let's try sums. We see that 10 + 10 = 20; 10 + 20 = 30; and 20 + 30 = 50. So we find the pattern of the series at last: the sum of any two consecutive numbers in the series is the same as the next number in the series. So the right answer should be 30 + 50. **Therefore the right answer is B. 80.**

10. As always, first let's find the differences between consecutive numbers. We see the gaps are: +6, −5, +8, −5. If this were the pattern, the next number should be 7 + 10 = 17. But 17 is not one of the answer choices. Next we see that we cannot solve it using ratios alone because neither 9/4 nor 4/9 is an integer. So let's combine differences and ratios together. Now we see that the gaps are: ×3, −5, ×3, −5. So the next answer should be 7 × 3. **So the right answer is K. 21.**

11. We see that the numerators have a constant gap of +2. We also see that the denominators have a constant gap of ×2. So the next number should be (9 + 2) / (32 × 2). **So the right answer is C. 11/64.**

12. Again, let's find the differences between consecutive numbers and see if we can uncover the pattern of the series this way. We see the gaps are: +10, −2, +10, −2. So the next number should be 43 + 10. **Therefore the right answer is M. 53.**

13. As before, let's find the differences between consecutive numbers. We see that the gaps are: +1, +3, +12, +90. There is no pattern here. We also find that ratios don't work because neither 2/3 nor 3/2 is an integer. Furthermore, we don't see any patterns of prime numbers or squares. Finally, let's try products. We see that 2 × 3 = 6; 3 × 6 = 18; and 6 ×18 = 108. So we find the pattern of the series at last: the product of any two consecutive

numbers in the series is the same as the next number in the series. So the right answer should be 18×108. **So the right answer is A. 1944.**

14. Many times the simplest thing is the best as well. Let's find the differences between consecutive numbers. We see the gaps are: +6, +6, +6, +6. So the next number should be $29 + 6$. **So the right answer is L. 35.**

15. Let's give it a try to find the differences between consecutive numbers. We see the gaps are: −2, +9, −2, +16. There is no pattern here. Next we find that we cannot use ratios alone because neither 11/9 nor 9/11 is an integer. So let's combine differences and ratios together. Now we see that the gaps are: −2, ×2, −2, ×2. So the next number should be $32 − 2$. **So the right answer is C. 30.**

16. As a first step, let's find the differences between consecutive numbers. We see the gaps are: +5, +7, +9, +11. So the next number should be $36 + 13$. **So the right answer is K. 49.**

17. As always, we check the differences between consecutive numbers. We see the gaps are: +1, +2, +3, +5. There is no pattern here. Next we find that ratios also don't work because neither 2/3 nor 3/2 is an integer. Moreover, we don't see any patterns of prime numbers or squares. Finally let's check sums. We see that $2 + 3 = 5$; $3 + 5 = 8$; and $5 + 8 = 13$. In fact, this series is the famous **Fibonacci numbers** in which the sum of any two consecutive numbers in the series is equal to the next number in the series. So the right answer should be $8 + 13$. **So the right answer is C. 21.**

18. First thing first, let's find the differences between consecutive numbers. We see that the gaps are: −10, −9, −8, −7. So the next number should be $21 − 6$. **So the right answer is L. 15.**

Part Three

Nonverbal

Chapter 19

Figure Matrices Traps and Tips

There are two types of questions in the figure matrices subarea: figure analogy and pattern completion. First let's look at a figure analogy question.

1.

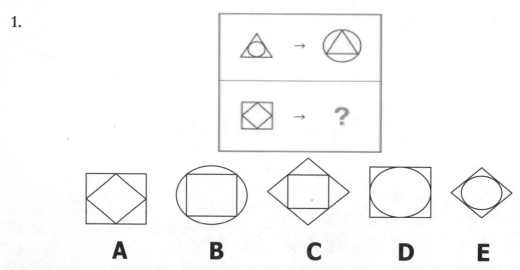

Like in verbal reasoning, the Trapdog is confident that you'll make inferences associatively rather than logically. One trick he likes to play in figure analogies is to use an answer picture that looks like the figure in the bottom row before the question mark as bait. Answer A is this type of bait.

Ha ha! I bet you can't even remember as far back as verbal analogies! You're as good as failed already! You won't get away this time! Mwua ha ha ha!

Like in verbal analogies, you need to make a **bridge rule** to describe the relationship between the two pictures in the top row. Remember that in case more than one answer picture fits your bridge rule, then you need to examine the first two pictures more closely and make a more precise bridge rule. In this example, you observe that in the top row an oval is inside a triangle in the first picture, but in the second picture an oval is outside a triangle. So your bridge rule might be: the change from the first to the second picture is that the inner shape and the outer shape switch positions with each other.

Now let's apply this rule to the bottom row. The first picture here is a rhombus inside a square. Applying the bridge rule, the missing picture should be a rhombus outside a square. Examining the answer choices, we see that **Answer C is correct.**

Tip: For figure analogies, make a bridge rule to describe the relationship between the figures. Think logically!

Now let's look at a pattern completion example.

2.

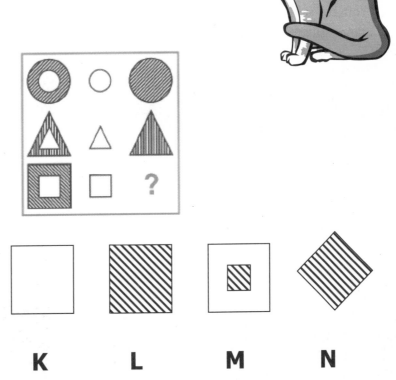

J   K   L   M   N

Tip: For pattern completion, not only think of a rule, but also put the rule into words and say it silently to yourself. This way your rule will be more precise and you will also remember it better.

We see that in the top row the shades are all slanted to the left. In the middle row the shades are all vertical. The shade of the left figure in the bottom row is slanted to the right. So the shade of the correct answer figure should be slanted to the right.

Next we see that in the top row there are two circles with the same center, one small circle, and one large circle. In the middle row, we see two triangles with the same center, one small triangle, and one large triangle. In the bottom row, we see two squares with the same center, one small square. So the missing figure should be a large square, and its shade should be slanted to the right. **So the right answer is L.**

That little cat! He foiled my plan again! He told you my secrets *and* how to avoid them. GRRRR! He's going to pay when I catch him!! But I'm running out of time! There are only two sections left!

Chapter 20

Figure Matrices Practice Test

(22 questions, 10 minutes)

In the Figure Matrices subtest, each question is a matrix or grid divided into sections. Each section contains either a shape, or a figure, or a question mark. Students must determine which of the available answers would best replace the question mark to complete the matrix. Questions usually come in two types: Figure Analogy or Pattern Completion.

1.

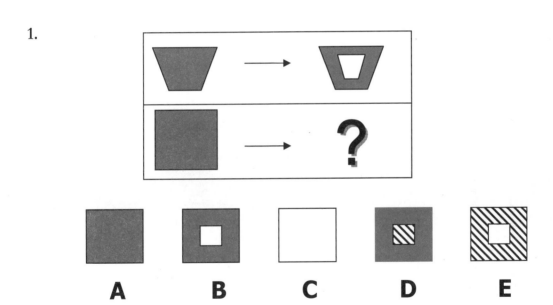

2.

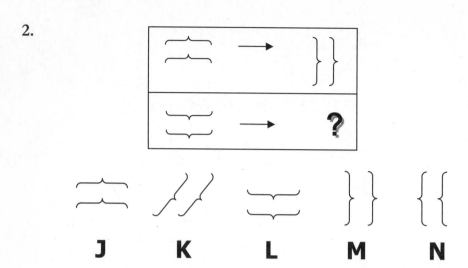

J   K   L   M   N

3.

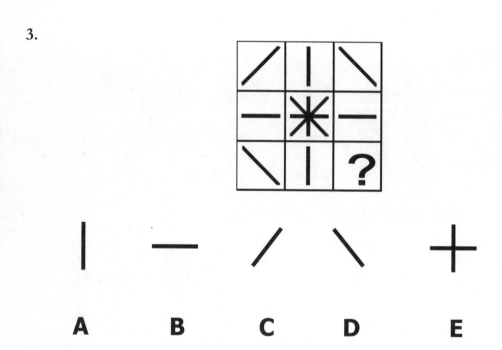

A   B   C   D   E

4.

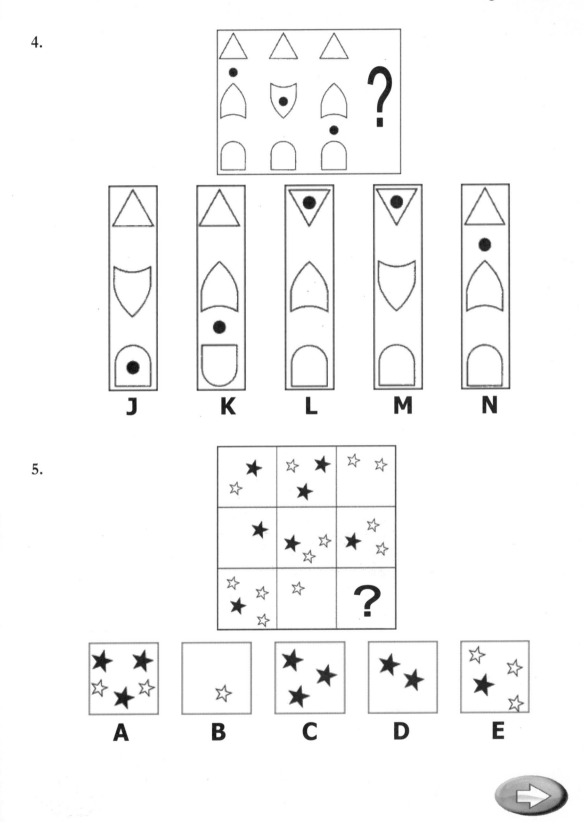

5.

6.

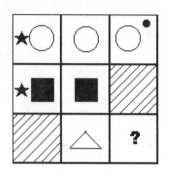

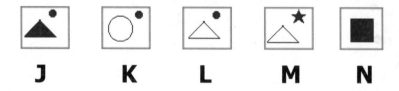

J   K   L   M   N

7.

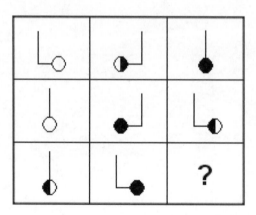

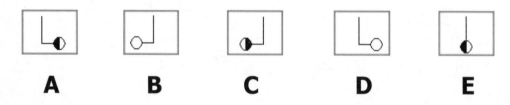

A   B   C   D   E

8.

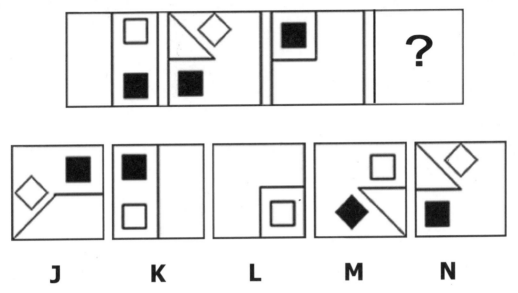

J   K   L   M   N

9.

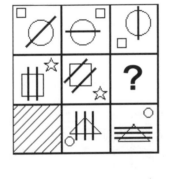

A   B   C   D   E

10.

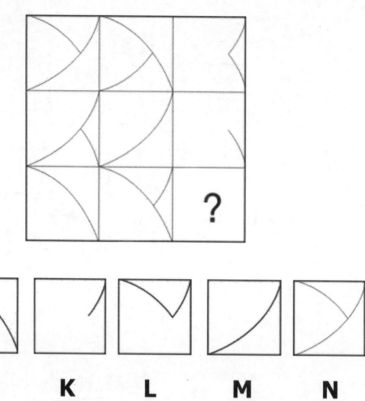

J   K   L   M   N

11.

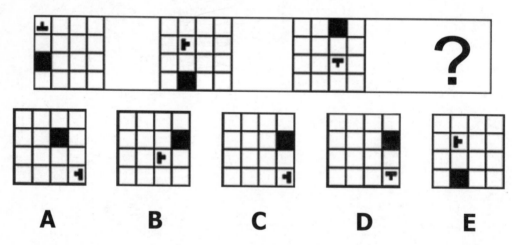

A   B   C   D   E

12.

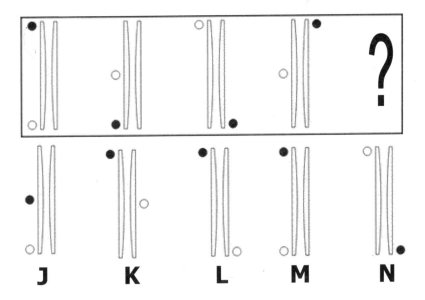

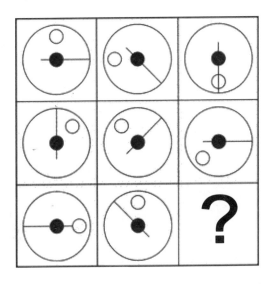

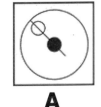 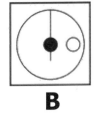 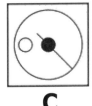 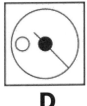 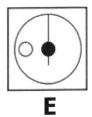

J **K** **L** **M** **N**

13.

A **B** **C** **D** **E**

14.

15.

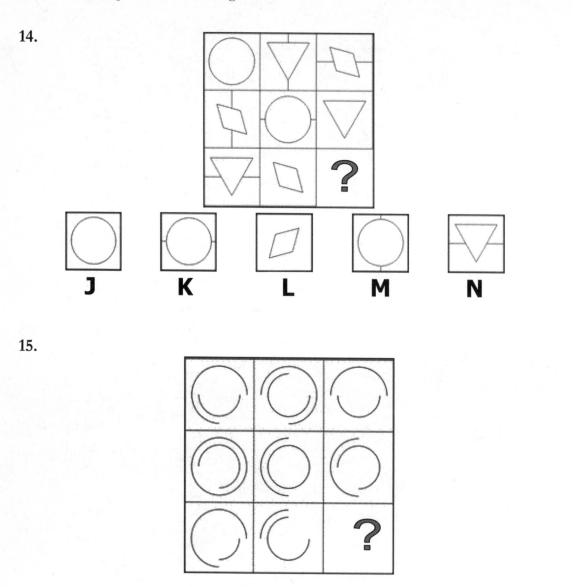

16.

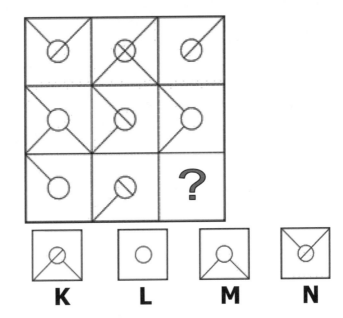

17.

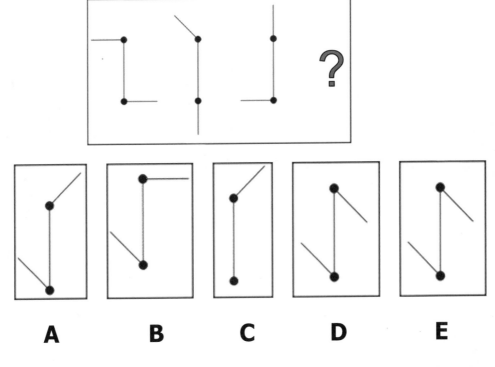

18.

J   K   L   M   N

19.

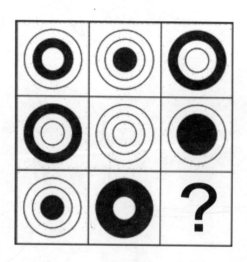

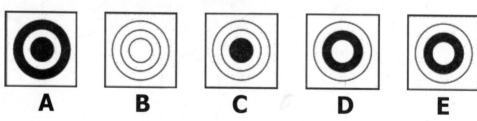

A   B   C   D   E

20.

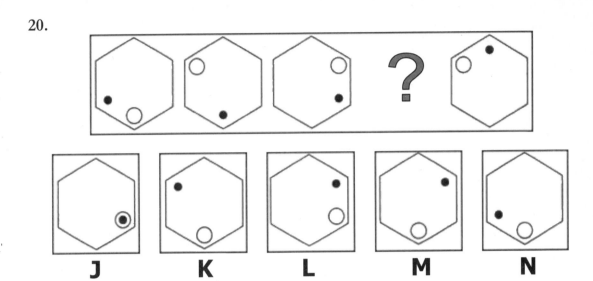

21.

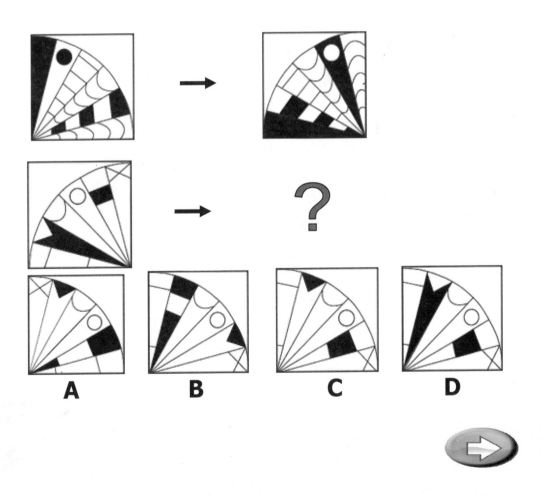

22.

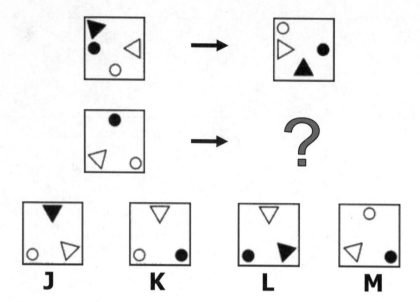

J   K   L   M

Nonverbal Battery Bubble Form

Figure Matrices

1. Ⓐ Ⓑ Ⓒ Ⓓ Ⓔ
2. Ⓙ Ⓚ Ⓛ Ⓜ Ⓝ
3. Ⓐ Ⓑ Ⓒ Ⓓ Ⓔ
4. Ⓙ Ⓚ Ⓛ Ⓜ Ⓝ
5. Ⓐ Ⓑ Ⓒ Ⓓ Ⓔ
6. Ⓙ Ⓚ Ⓛ Ⓜ Ⓝ
7. Ⓐ Ⓑ Ⓒ Ⓓ Ⓔ
8. Ⓙ Ⓚ Ⓛ Ⓜ Ⓝ
9. Ⓐ Ⓑ Ⓒ Ⓓ Ⓔ
10. Ⓙ Ⓚ Ⓛ Ⓜ Ⓝ
11. Ⓐ Ⓑ Ⓒ Ⓓ Ⓔ
12. Ⓙ Ⓚ Ⓛ Ⓜ Ⓝ
13. Ⓐ Ⓑ Ⓒ Ⓓ Ⓔ
14. Ⓙ Ⓚ Ⓛ Ⓜ Ⓝ
15. Ⓐ Ⓑ Ⓒ Ⓓ Ⓔ
16. Ⓙ Ⓚ Ⓛ Ⓜ Ⓝ
17. Ⓐ Ⓑ Ⓒ Ⓓ Ⓔ
18. Ⓙ Ⓚ Ⓛ Ⓜ Ⓝ
19. Ⓐ Ⓑ Ⓒ Ⓓ Ⓔ
20. Ⓙ Ⓚ Ⓛ Ⓜ Ⓝ
21. Ⓐ Ⓑ Ⓒ Ⓓ
22. Ⓙ Ⓚ Ⓛ Ⓜ

Paper Folding

1. Ⓐ Ⓑ Ⓒ Ⓓ Ⓔ
2. Ⓙ Ⓚ Ⓛ Ⓜ Ⓝ
3. Ⓐ Ⓑ Ⓒ Ⓓ Ⓔ
4. Ⓙ Ⓚ Ⓛ Ⓜ Ⓝ
5. Ⓐ Ⓑ Ⓒ Ⓓ Ⓔ
6. Ⓙ Ⓚ Ⓛ Ⓜ Ⓝ
7. Ⓐ Ⓑ Ⓒ Ⓓ Ⓔ
8. Ⓙ Ⓚ Ⓛ Ⓜ Ⓝ
9. Ⓐ Ⓑ Ⓒ Ⓓ Ⓔ
10. Ⓙ Ⓚ Ⓛ Ⓜ Ⓝ
11. Ⓐ Ⓑ Ⓒ Ⓓ Ⓔ
12. Ⓙ Ⓚ Ⓛ Ⓜ Ⓝ
13. Ⓐ Ⓑ Ⓒ Ⓓ Ⓔ
14. Ⓙ Ⓚ Ⓛ Ⓜ Ⓝ
15. Ⓐ Ⓑ Ⓒ Ⓓ Ⓔ
16. Ⓙ Ⓚ Ⓛ Ⓜ Ⓝ

Figure Classification

1. Ⓐ Ⓑ Ⓒ Ⓓ Ⓔ
2. Ⓙ Ⓚ Ⓛ Ⓜ Ⓝ
3. Ⓐ Ⓑ Ⓒ Ⓓ Ⓔ
4. Ⓙ Ⓚ Ⓛ Ⓜ Ⓝ
5. Ⓐ Ⓑ Ⓒ Ⓓ Ⓔ
6. Ⓙ Ⓚ Ⓛ Ⓜ Ⓝ
7. Ⓐ Ⓑ Ⓒ Ⓓ Ⓔ
8. Ⓙ Ⓚ Ⓛ Ⓜ Ⓝ
9. Ⓐ Ⓑ Ⓒ Ⓓ Ⓔ
10. Ⓙ Ⓚ Ⓛ Ⓜ Ⓝ
11. Ⓐ Ⓑ Ⓒ Ⓓ Ⓔ
12. Ⓙ Ⓚ Ⓛ Ⓜ Ⓝ
13. Ⓐ Ⓑ Ⓒ Ⓓ Ⓔ
14. Ⓙ Ⓚ Ⓛ Ⓜ Ⓝ
15. Ⓐ Ⓑ Ⓒ Ⓓ Ⓔ
16. Ⓙ Ⓚ Ⓛ Ⓜ Ⓝ
17. Ⓐ Ⓑ Ⓒ Ⓓ Ⓔ
18. Ⓙ Ⓚ Ⓛ Ⓜ Ⓝ
19. Ⓐ Ⓑ Ⓒ Ⓓ Ⓔ
20. Ⓙ Ⓚ Ⓛ Ⓜ Ⓝ
21. Ⓐ Ⓑ Ⓒ Ⓓ Ⓔ
22. Ⓙ Ⓚ Ⓛ Ⓜ Ⓝ

Chapter 21

Figure Matrices Test Solutions

I recommend that you read through these solutions carefully even when you get the right answer. They might give you some insight into how to solve real CogAT problems.

1. Here in the first row the left side shape is a gray trapezoid and the right side shape is a gray trapezoid with a smaller white trapezoid inside it. In the second row, we see a gray square. So the correct answer should be a gray square with a smaller white square inside it. **So the right answer is B.**

2. In this problem we see a pair of brackets gets rotated 90 degrees clockwise in the first row. So the correct answer should be the left side figure in the second row gets rotated 90 degrees clockwise. **So the right answer is N.**

3. This is a pattern completion problem. We see that the matrix has rotational symmetry. **So the right answer is C.**

4. We notice that in the top row it is the same shape in every column. In the middle row, the shape gets flipped horizontally from column to column. The shape in the bottom row is the same in each column. Also we notice that a black dot travels downward through the columns. We see that only Answer J fits all these patterns. **So the right answer is J.**

5. Inspecting the top row, we see that there are three dark stars and four light-colored stars in total. Also we notice 3 dark stars and 4 light-colored stars in the middle row. In the first two figures of the bottom row, there are 1 black star and 4 light-colored stars. To complete the pattern, we need two more black stars and no more white. **So the right answer is D.**

6. In this type of question, a square with slanted shades means that the figure is blocked from view. So we can replace it with a figure that fits the pattern. In the top row, we see a star with a circle, a plain circle, and a circle with a black dot. In the middle row, we see a star with a black square, a plain black square, and a blocked figure. Based on the pattern in the top row, this

blocked figure is a black square with a black dot. In the third row, we see a blocked figure, a plain triangle, and a question mark. Continuing the pattern, the blocked figure in the third row is a star with a triangle, and the question mark is a triangle with a black dot. **So the right answer is L.**

7. First let's observe the pattern of the circles. In the top row we see a white circle, a half-white circle, and a black circle. This pattern continues in the middle row. In the third row, we see a half-white circle and a black circle. So the right answer must have a white circle. Next let's observe the line pattern. In the top row there is a "L", a flipped to the left "L", and a vertical line. This pattern continues in the middle row. In the bottom row, we see a vertical line and a "L". So the right answer must have a flipped to the left "L". **So the right answer is B.**

8. Examining the pattern of the black square, we see that it moves from the bottom right corner in the first picture to the bottom left corner in the second picture to the top left corner in the third picture. To complete the pattern, it should be in the top right corner in the fourth picture. We notice that only answer choice J has a black square in the top right corner. **So the right answer is J.**

9. In the top row we see a small square and a circle in each picture. In the second row we see a small star and a square in each of the first two pictures. So the missing picture must have a star and a square. Next let's examine the line pattern. In the top row, the line is rotated 45 degrees clockwise from the first to the second picture. Next it is rotated 90 degrees clockwise from the second to the third picture. We see that in the middle row a pair of parallel lines gets rotated 45 degrees clockwise from the first to the second picture. To complete the pattern, the missing picture must have this pair of parallel lines rotated 90 degrees clockwise from its position in the second picture. We see that only answer choice D fits all these patterns. **So the right answer is D.**

10. This is a line reduction problem. We see that the last picture in the top row consists of lines that appear only once in either the first or the second picture of the top row. This pattern continues in the second row. So to complete the pattern, the missing picture must consist of lines that appear only once in either the first or the second picture in the bottom row. **So the right answer is K.**

11. First let's check the pattern of the black square. It moves one grid to the right each time. So Answers A and E are ruled out. Next let's check the pattern of "⊥". It moves downward and to the right and gets rotated 90 degrees clockwise each time. Examining the remaining answer choices B, C, and D, we see that only C fits all these patterns. **So the right answer is C.**

12. Looking at the white circle, we see that it's always at the left side of the two long sticks. It goes from the bottom to the middle to the top. Then it goes back to the middle again. To continue the pattern, the white circle must be at the bottom left side of the two sticks in the missing picture. So Answers K, L, and N are ruled out. Next let's check the pattern of the black circle. It goes from the top left corner to the bottom left corner of the two long sticks. Next it goes to the bottom right corner, and then to the top right corner. To complete the pattern, the black circle must be at the top left corner of the two long sticks in the missing picture. So Answer J is ruled out. **So the right answer is M.**

13. We see that in the top row the black handle moves 45 degrees clockwise each time. This pattern continues in the second and the third row. To complete the pattern, the black handle should be pointing to the top in the missing figure. So Answers A, C, and D are ruled out. Next let's look at the white circle. It rotates 90 degrees counter clockwise each time in the top row. This pattern continues in the second row. We see the white circle rotates 90 degrees counter clockwise from the first to the second figure in the bottom row. To complete the pattern, the white circle must be at the middle left side of the missing figure. So Answer B is ruled out. **So the right answer is E.**

14. In both the top and the middle row, we see a circle, a triangle, and a rhombus. We see a triangle and a rhombus in the first two pictures of the bottom row. To complete the pattern, we must have a circle in the missing picture. So Answers L and N are ruled out. We see a horizontal line and a vertical line in the top and the middle row. We see a horizontal line in the bottom row. To complete the pattern, the missing picture must have a vertical line. So Answers J and K are ruled out. **So the right answer is M.**

15. Again this is a line reduction problem. But unlike Problem 10, here the last picture of the top row consists of curves that are common in both the first and the second picture in the top row. This pattern continues in the middle row. To complete the pattern, the missing picture must consist of curves

that are common in both the first and the second picture of the bottom row. **So the right answer is E.**

16. Like Problem 15, this is a line reduction problem in which the last picture of each row consists of lines that are common in both the first and the second picture of that row. To complete the pattern, the missing picture must have a circle and nothing more than a circle. **So the right answer is L.**

17. Here we see that the top line segment rotates 45 degrees clockwise each time. We also see that the bottom line segment rotates 90 degrees clockwise each time. The only answer choice that fits these patterns is C. **So the right answer is C.**

18. In the first part, we see 3 circles, two square brackets, and a triangle. In the second part, we see 3 triangles and two parentheses. To complete the pattern, the missing figure must have only one shape. So Answers J and N are ruled out. Next we observe that from 3 circles to 3 triangles, the shapes are changed from curves to straight lines. From 2 square brackets to 2 parentheses, the shapes are changed from straight lines to curves. Since the counterpart of the missing figure is a triangle with straight lines, the missing figure must have curves. So Answers K and M are ruled out. **So the right answer is L.**

19. Here we see that combining all the shades together in the top row, we have a completely shaded large circle. This pattern continues in the middle row. Since the shades combined from the first two pictures of the bottom row form a completely shaded large circle already, the missing picture must have no shades at all. **Therefore the right answer is B.**

20. We see that the white circle rotates 120 degrees clockwise each time. So the missing picture must have this white circle in the bottom of the hexagon. So Answers J and L are ruled out. We also notice that the black dot rotates 60 degrees counter clockwise each time. So Answers K and N are ruled out. **So the right answer is M.**

21. This is a figure analogy problem. Let's look at the pictures in the top row. There are six shapes in each picture. We see that the first shape and the sixth shape in the first picture get swapped in the second picture. The shades of the second and the fifth shape are exactly the opposite in the first and the second picture. Also we see that the third and the fourth shape in

the first picture get swapped in the second picture. Applying these patterns to the first picture in the bottom row, **we see that the right answer is B.**

22. This is a figure substitution problem. In the top row, we see that from the first to the second picture, the black circle is replaced with the white triangle; the white triangle is replaced with the black circle; the black triangle is replaced with the white circle; and the white circle is replaced with the black triangle. Applying these patterns to the first picture in the bottom row, **we see that the right answer is L.**

Chapter 22

Paper Folding Traps and Tips

Paper folding is my favorite! You ignorant little kids don't know how many holes there are! I'll make you crazy wrong with my traps this time!!

Like number puzzles, there are only 16 questions in the paper folding subtest. That means it's one of the two hardest subtests in CogAT. So we need to use good thinking here. In order to identify strategies students use in the paper folding test, Hegarty Spatial Thinking Lab asked test takers to think aloud while solving test problems.* Dr. Hegarty found that many good test takers "started at the last step shown and worked backward to unfold the paper and see where the holes would be." In addition to this imagery strategy, some students also used analytic strategies such as figuring out how many layers of paper were punched through and therefore how many holes there would be in the paper at the end. According to this study, "students who reported determining the number of holes in the final answer choice had significantly higher scores on the test than those who did not report using this strategy."

* Hegarty, M. (2010). Components of Spatial Intelligence. In B. H. Ross (Ed.) *The Psychology of Learning and Motivation, Vol. 52*. San Diego: Academic Press (pp. 265–297).

Tip: For paper folding, count the number of layers of paper that are punched through to determine how many holes there should be.

Let's assume that a maximum of 4 × 4 holes could be punched in a piece of square paper because the same strategy can be applied to other cases with more than 16 or fewer than 16 holes. Let's borrow chess notations to identify these 16 positions as shown in the figure below. We call the holes in the last row A1, B1, C1, and D1. We call the holes in the second to last row A2, B2, C2, and D2, etc.

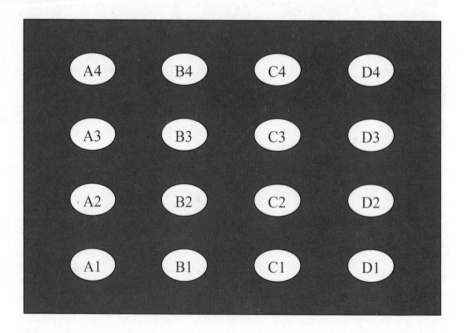

Now let's look at an example.

1.

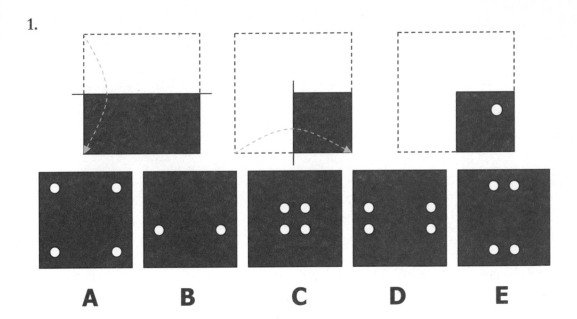

The paper is folded twice. Each fold doubles the number of the holes. So there should be four holes in total. So Answer B is ruled out. Next we identify the location of the original hole. We see that location D2 of the paper is punched. Unfolding the second fold, we get one more hole in location A2. Unfolding the first fold, we get two more holes in locations A3 and D3. **Therefore the right answer is D.**

Now let's look at another example.

2.

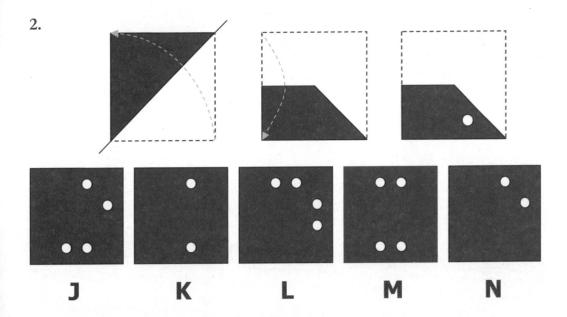

Some people use a quick but unreliable strategy to solve paper folding problems. They first note the location of where the hole is punched. Next they check the answer choices to see if there are any choices that do not have a hole in this location and eliminate these answer choices. This strategy almost always works because there is usually a hole in the location at which the hole is originally punched after the unfolding process. But this strategy does not work 100% of the time. The problem we are working on now is such an example.

To solve this problem, first let's determine how many holes are punched. The paper is folded twice, but after the first fold nothing is there in location C1 where the original hole is punched. So there are only two layers of paper that are punched through and therefore only two holes in total. So Answers J, L, and M are ruled out.

Next let's unfold the second and also the last fold of the paper. **This moves the original hole in location C1 to a hole in location C4.** Finally we unfold the first fold and get a second hole in location D3. **So the right answer is N.**

Chapter 23

Paper Folding Practice Test

(16 questions, 10 minutes)

In the Paper Folding subtest, each question shows a square piece of paper being folded and then the folded paper is hole-punched. Select the answer from the bottom row that shows how the folded paper with holes will look when it is unfolded.

1.

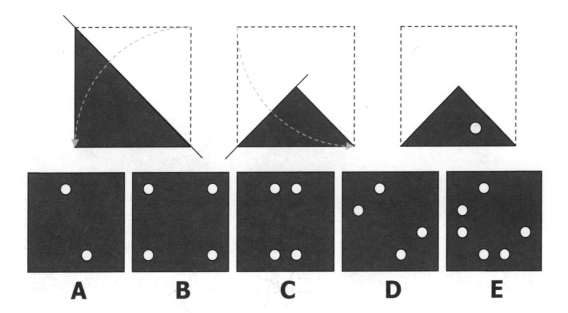

2.

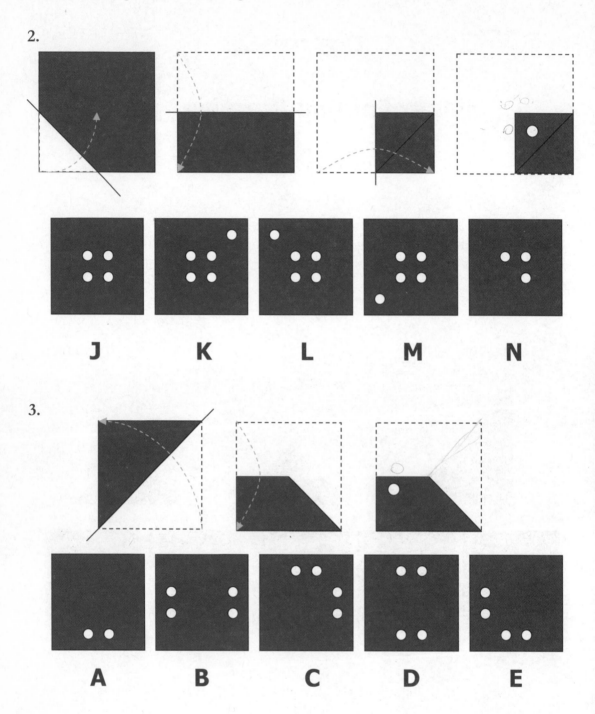

J   K   L   M   N

3.

A   B   C   D   E

4.

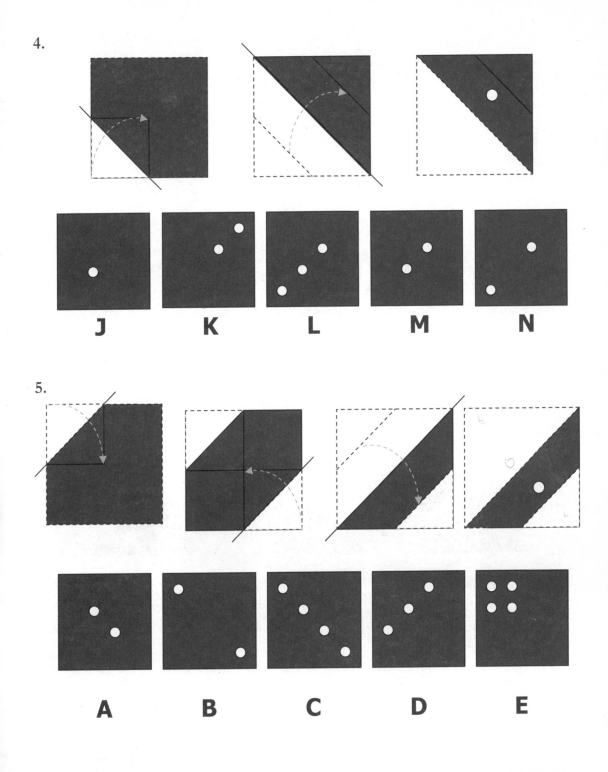

J K L M N

5.

A B C D E

6.

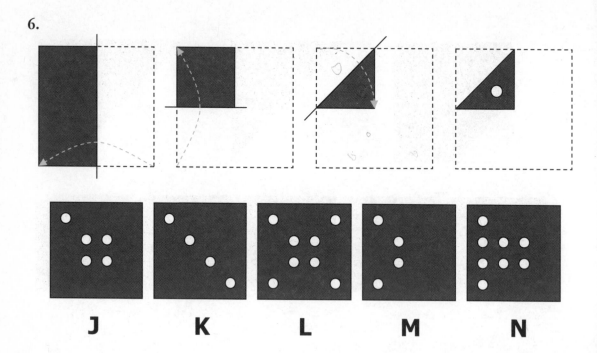

J   K   L   M   N

7.

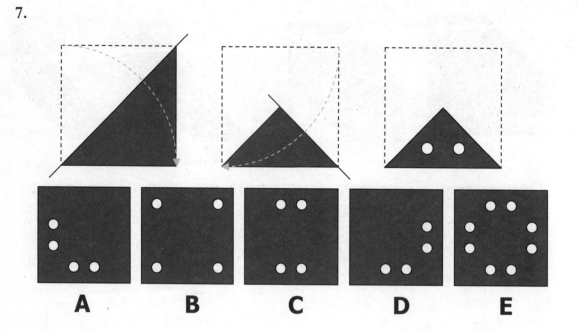

A   B   C   D   E

8.

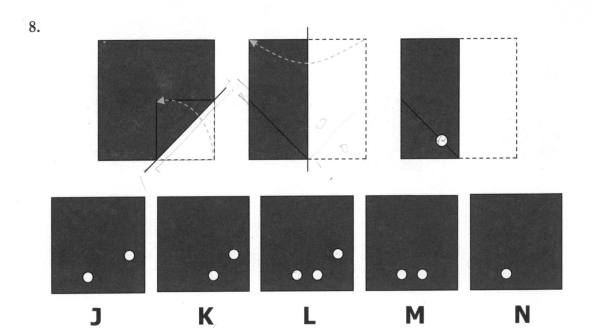

| J | K | L | M | N |

9.

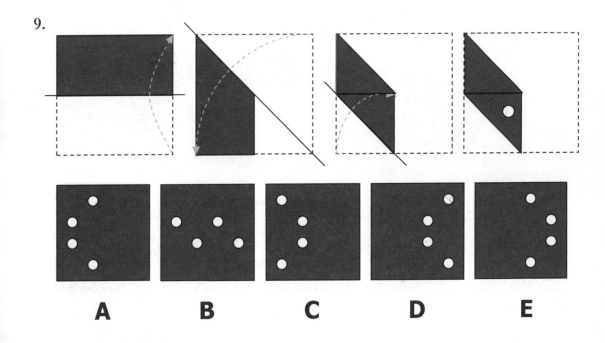

| A | B | C | D | E |

10.

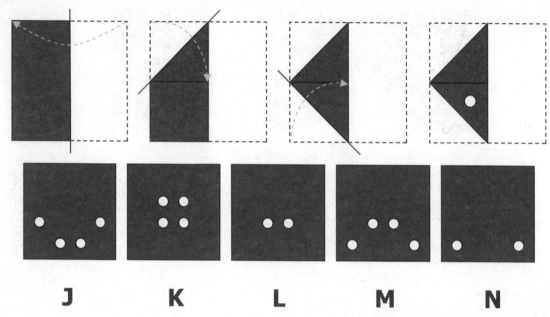

J K L M N

11.

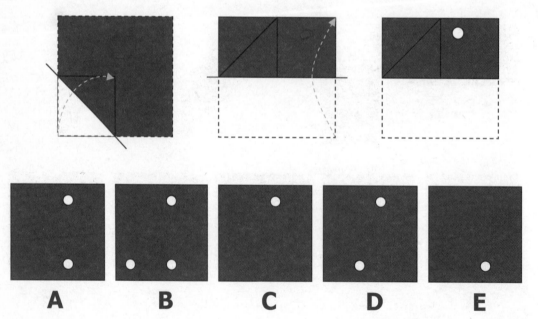

A B C D E

12.

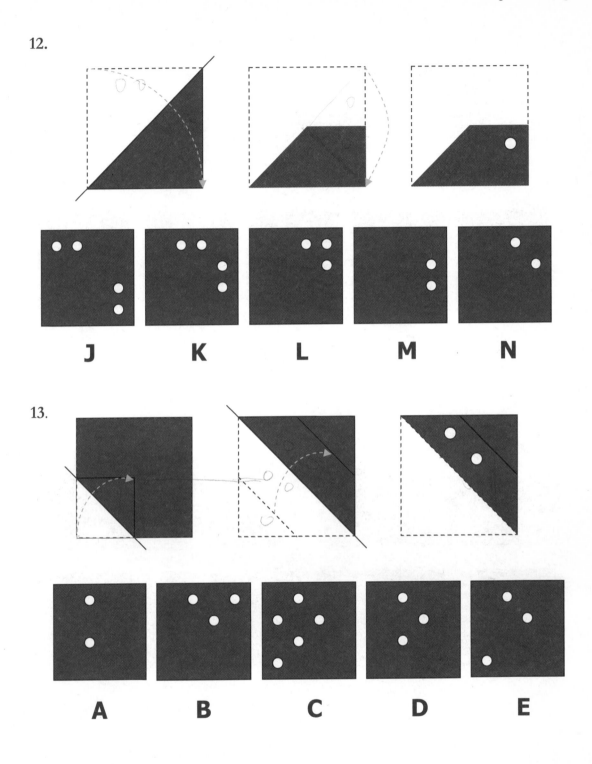

J   **K**   **L**   **M**   **N**

13.

A   **B**   **C**   **D**   **E**

14.

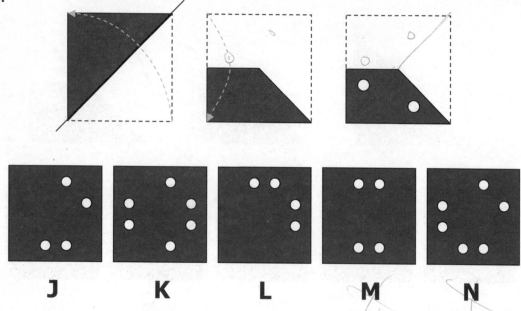

15.

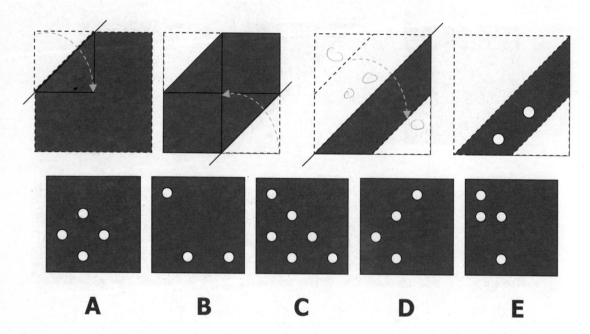

16.

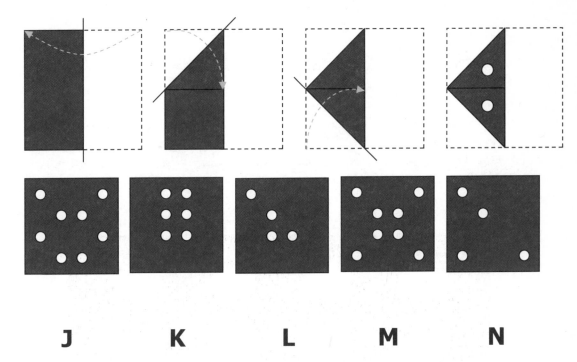

J   K   L   M   N

Chapter 24

Paper Folding Test Solutions

I recommend that you read through these solutions carefully even when you get the right answer. They might give you some insight into how to solve real CogAT problems. I include the chess notation figure here one more time so that you can easily follow my explanations.

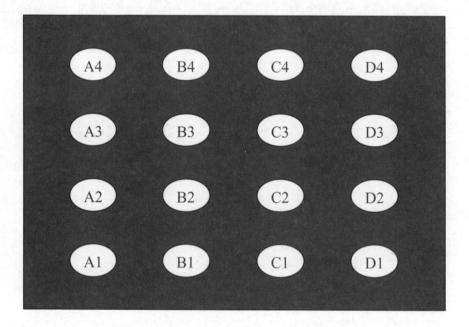

1. In this problem the paper is folded twice. In total there are four layers of paper that are punched through. So there should be four holes in the unfolded paper. So Answers A and E are ruled out. The original hole is in location C1. We unfold the second fold and get one more hole in location A3. Finally we unfold the first fold and get two more holes in locations B4 and D2. **So the right answer is D.**

2. The paper is folded three times in this problem. The hole is punched in location C2. Unfolding the last fold, we get one more hole in location B2. Unfolding the second fold, we get two more holes in locations B3 and C3. Fi-

nally we unfold the first fold and get the last hole in location A1. **So the right answer is M.**

3. Here the paper is folded twice and in total four layers of paper are punched through. So there should be four holes in the unfolded paper. So Answer A is ruled out. The original hole is in location A2. Unfolding the second fold, we get one more hole in location A3. Unfolding the first fold, we get two more holes in locations B1 and C1. **So the right answer is E.**

4. The hole is punched in location C3 in this problem. There are two folds in total. Unfolding the second fold, we get one more hole in location B2. Unfolding the first fold, we get the last hole in location A1. **So the right answer is L.**

5. In this problem the paper is folded three times and the original hole is in location C2. We see that there are in total four layers of paper that are punched through. So there are four holes in the unfolded paper. So Answers A, B, and D are ruled out. Unfolding the last fold, we get one more hole in location B3. Unfolding the second fold, we get one more hole in location D1. Finally we unfold the first fold and get the last hole in location A4. **So the right answer is C.**

6. Here the paper is folded three times and there are eight layers of paper that are punched through. So Answers J, K, and M are ruled out. The paper is punched in location B3. Unfolding the last fold, we get one more hole in location A4. Unfolding the second fold, we get two more holes in locations A1 and B2. Finally we unfold the first fold and get four more holes in locations D1, C2, C3, and D4. **So the right answer is L.**

7. We have two holes punched in this problem. They are in locations B1 and C1. The paper is folded twice. So we have eight holes in total in the unfolded paper. Unfolding the second fold, we get two more holes in locations D2 and D3. Unfolding the first fold, we get four more holes in locations A2, A3, B4, and C4. **So the right answer is E.**

8. This is a tricky problem because the hole is punched right on a fold in location B1. There are two folds in total here. Unfolding the second fold, we get half of a hole in location C1. Unfolding the first fold, we get the other half of the hole in location C1. **So the right answer is M.**

9. Although the paper is folded three times in this problem, only four layers of paper are punched through. Furthermore, nothing is there in the location of the original Hole B2 after the first fold. So this is really a tricky problem. To solve it, let's first unfold the last fold. We get holes in locations A1 and B2. Unfolding the second fold, we see that these two holes are now **moved** to locations C3 and D4. Finally we unfold the first fold and get two more holes in locations C2 and D1. **So the right answer is D.**

10. In this problem the paper is folded three times but there are only four layers of paper that are punched through. The hole is punched in location B2. Unfolding the last fold, we get one more hole in location A1. Unfolding the second fold, we get no more holes. Unfolding the first fold, we get two more holes in locations C2 and D1. **So the right answer is M.**

11. Here the paper is folded twice but there are only two layers of paper that are punched through. The original hole is in location C4. Unfolding the last fold, we get one more hole in location C1. Unfolding the first fold, we do not get any more holes. **So the right answer is A.**

12. The paper is folded twice. The hole is punched in location D2. Unfolding the second fold, we get one more hole in location D3. Unfolding the first fold, we get two more holes in locations B4 and C4. **Therefore the right answer is K.**

13. The paper is folded twice in this problem. The original holes are punched in locations B4 and C3. Unfolding the second fold, we get two more holes in locations A3 and B2. Unfolding the first fold, we get one more hole in location A1. **So the right answer is C.**

14. In this problem the paper is folded twice. The original holes are punched in locations A2 and C1. These two holes are punched through different layers of the paper so let's examine them one by one. First let's look at Hole A2. Unfolding the second fold, we get one more hole in location A3. Unfolding the first fold, we get two more holes in locations B1 and C1. Now let's look at Hole C1. Note that there is nothing in location C1 after the first fold, so there are only two layers of paper that are punched though in this location. Unfolding the second fold, this hole is **moved** to location C4. Unfolding the first fold, we get one more hole in location D3. Combining all these holes together, **we see that the right answer is N.**

15. Here the paper is folded three times. The original holes are punched in locations B1 and C2. First let's look at Hole B1. Unfolding the last fold, we get one more hole in location A2. Unfolding the second and the first fold, we do not get any more holes. Now let's look at Hole C2. Unfolding the last fold, we get one more hole in location B3. Unfolding the second fold, we get one more hole in location D1. Unfolding the first fold, we get the last hole in location A4. Combining all these holes, **we see that the right answer is C.**

16. Again this paper is folded three times. The original holes are punched in locations B2 and B3. Unfolding the last fold, we get one more hole in location A1. Unfolding the second fold, we get one more hole in location A4. Unfolding the first fold, we get four more holes in locations D1, C2, C3, and D4. **So the right answer is M.**

Chapter 25

Figure Classification Traps and Tips

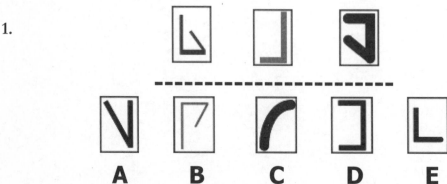

We children stumble over bubble forms from time to time. The most costly problem is that sometimes we skip a line and mark our answer in the wrong place. This single error causes all the answers after that being marked in the wrong places. Even if we are lucky enough to find out the original error before the end of the test, erasing all the errors and marking all the answers again takes away precious test time, not to say all the frustrations it brings. Fortunately, this problem can be avoided. A good solution is to use a blank 3" by 5" index card. You can use it to line up the question number together with the answer choices for this question so that you always know which question you are answering. Now let's get back to the topic of this chapter, figure classification. Like verbal classification, we need to find a rule to describe the similarities among the three pictures in the top row. Sometimes two or more answer choices fit our rule. Then we have to go back to these three pictures again and find a more precise rule. Let's look at a figure classification question.

1.

At first glance, we see that all three figures in the top row have a right angle, so Answers A and C are ruled out. But which one among answer choices B, D, and E is the right answer? Looking more closely at the figures in the top row, we see that each figure has one and only one right angle. So Answer D is ruled out. Next we see that the two lines that form the right angle have different lengths in each figure of the top row. So Answer E is ruled out. **So the right answer is B.**

Now let's look at another typical question in figure classification, a rotation question. Remember that for this type of question, if you see both a rotation and a flip of the original shape, then the rotated shape is a better answer choice.

2.

J   K   L   M   N

> Tip: For figure classification, a rotated shape is a better answer choice than a flipped shape.

Examining the top row, we see that they are all the same shape rotated in some way. So we need to find a rotation of the same shape. We see that each of the answer choices J, K, M, and N is a rotation of the flipped original shape. So they are all ruled out. **Therefore the right answer is L.**

Chapter 26

Figure Classification Practice Test
(22 questions, 10 minutes)

In the Figure Classification subtest, each question has two rows of figures. In the top row, the student is given a set of three figures that are similar in some way. Students must determine how they are similar and then select the figure from the available answers that is most similar to the pictures in the top row.

1.

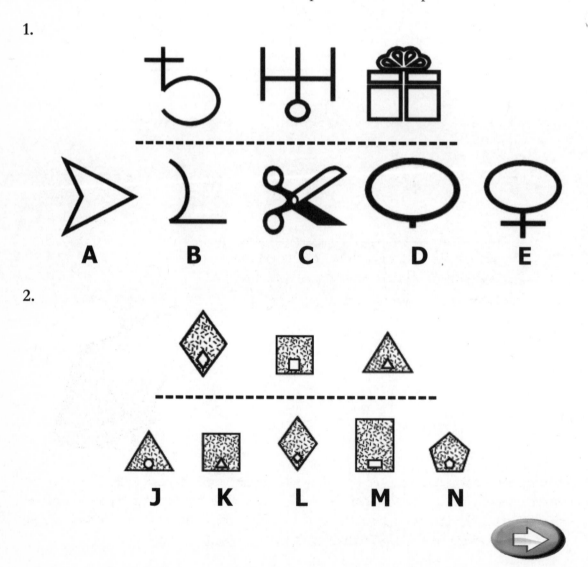

3.

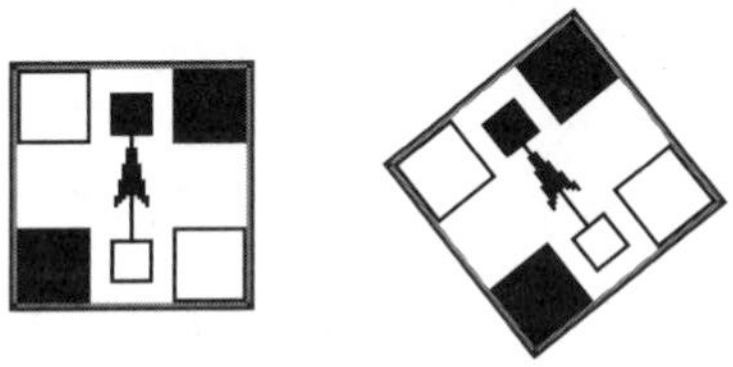

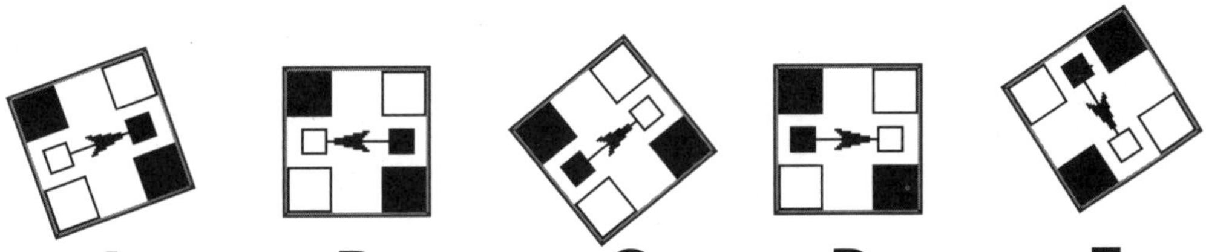

A   B   C   D   E

4.

J   K   L   M   N

5.

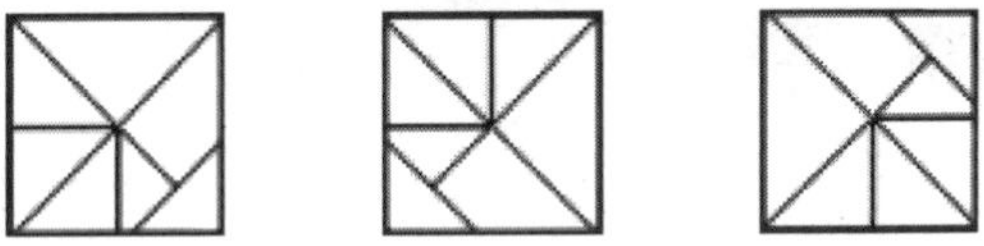

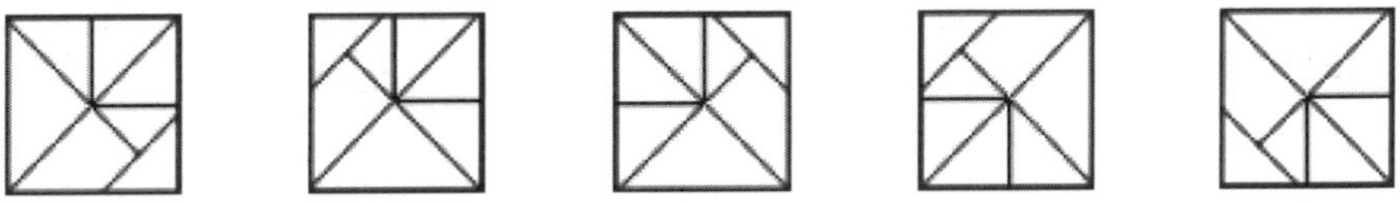

A   B   C   D   E

6.

J   **K**   **L**   **M**   **N**

7.

A   **B**   **C**   **D**   **E**

8.

J   **K**   **L**   **M**   **N**

9.

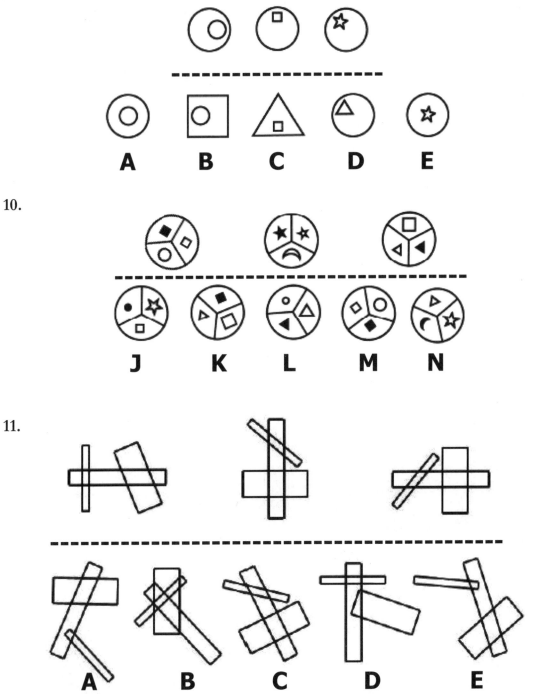

10.

11.

12.

13.

14.

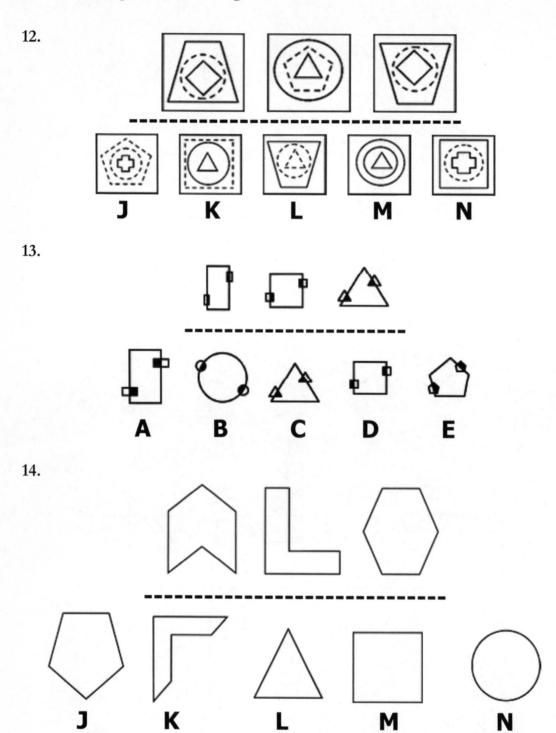

15.

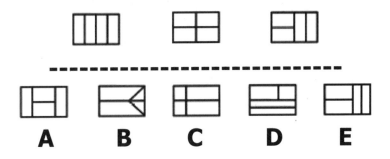

16.

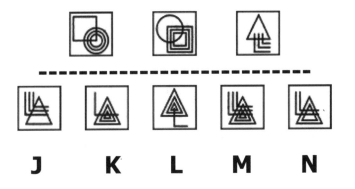

17.

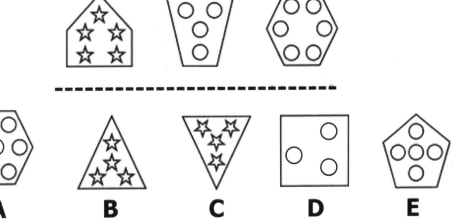

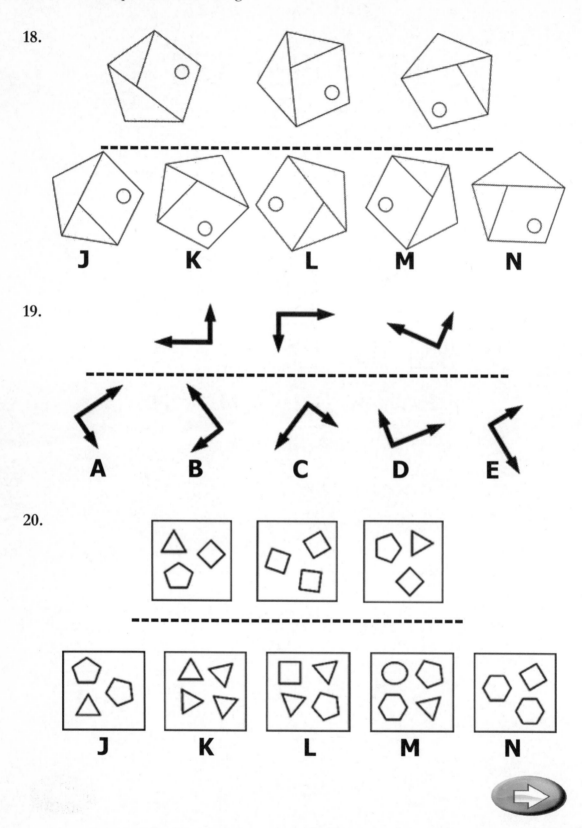
18.

19.

20.

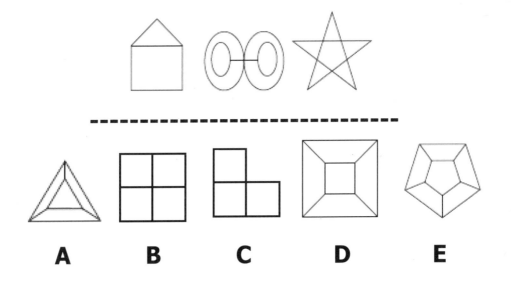

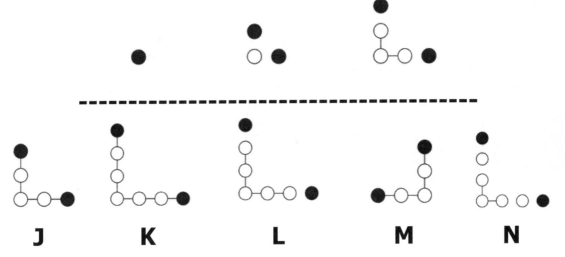

21.

A   B   C   D   E

22.

J   K   L   M   N

Chapter 27

Figure Classification Test Solutions

I recommend that you read through these solutions carefully even when you get the right answer. They might give you some insight into how to solve real CogAT problems.

1. At first glance, it's not easy to spot similarities among the three pictures in the top row. Looking more closely, we see that these three pictures all have one thing in common: each of them has two straight lines that are perpendicular to each other. So Answers A, B, C, and D are ruled out because there are no 90 degree angles in these answer choices. **So the correct answer is E.**

2. Examining the three pictures in the top row, we see that each picture has one large shape and one smaller but otherwise the same shape within the large shape. Answers J, K, and L are ruled out because for each of them, its large shape does not match its inner small shape. Answer M is ruled out because although both shapes are rectangles, these two rectangles are not proportional to each other. **So the right answer is N.**

3. We see here that all these three pictures in the top row are the same shape rotated in different ways. Note also that in each of these three pictures the direction of the arrow points from a white square to a black square. So Answers B, C, D, and E are ruled out because in each of these four pictures the arrow points from a black square to a white square. Only Answer A matches the pictures in the top row. **So the right answer is A.**

4. Let's treat one square as two triangles. Then we see that each of these three pictures in the top row has four black triangles. So Answers J, L, M, and N are ruled out because each of them has five black triangles. For Answer K, we see that its black quadrilateral is comprised of two black triangles. So it also has four black triangles. **Therefore the right answer is K.**

5. This is a rotation problem. Let's look at the three pictures in the top row. If we rotate each of them clockwise, we see that the large triangle is immediately followed by a small triangle. Answers A, C, D, and E are ruled out be-

cause when we do the same rotation to each of them, we see that the large triangle is not immediately followed by a small triangle. Only Answer B fits the pattern. **So the right answer is B.**

6. This is a tricky problem. Examining the three pictures in the top row, we do not see anything that they share in common. In such situations, it's a good idea to check the five answer choices and see if we might find something here. We see that all but one of the five answer pictures have a small inner shape that matches its large outer shape. Clearly this is not a characteristic of the top three pictures. Now we find what these three pictures in the top row have in common: they do not have matching inner and outer shapes. Therefore answer choices J, K, L, and M are ruled out. **The correct answer is N.**

7. This is a counting problem. We notice that each of these three pictures is divided into five parts. Examining the answer choices, we see that only answer picture E is divided into five parts. **So the right answer is E.**

8. We see that each picture in the top row consists of five shapes one on top of another with the smallest white shape on top of all. The shapes have alternating colors of either black or white. All five shapes are of the same kind but sequentially getting bigger and bigger. Answers J and M are ruled out because their shapes are not ordered according to sizes. Answer N is ruled out because its shapes are not of the same kind. Answer K is ruled out because its smallest shape is not on top of all. Only Answer L fits all the patterns of the pictures in the top row. **So the right answer is L.**

9. First we note that the outer shape of each of the three figures in the top row is a circle. So Answers B and C are ruled out. Next we observe that in the top row, none of the three small inner shapes is exactly located in the center of the large circle. So Answers A and E are ruled out. **So the right answer is D.**

10. Each picture in the top row has three small shapes. Among these three shapes, two of them are almost identical except that one is white and the other is black. Answers J and N are ruled out because each of them has three different shapes. Answers K and L are ruled out because for each of them, its black shape doesn't have the same size as its white counterpart. Only Answer M fits all the patterns of the pictures in the top row. **So the right answer is M.**

11. Examining the three pictures in the top row, we see that each has two rectangles perpendicular to each other. So Answers A, B, and E are ruled out. Furthermore, we notice that in every picture in the top row, the two overlapping but not perpendicular rectangles overlap with each other completely and the overlapped area forms a quadrilateral. So Answer D is ruled out. **So the right answer is C.**

12. Here in each of the three pictures in the top row, we see one and only one dotted shape. So Answers J, L, and M are ruled out. Furthermore, we notice that this dotted shape surrounds the smallest inner shape. So Answer K is ruled out. **Therefore the right answer is N.**

13. First we see that in each of the three pictures in the top row, the shaded shapes are within a larger shape. So Answers D and E are ruled out. Next we notice that none of the top pictures has curves. So Answer B is ruled out. Furthermore, we see that in each of the three pictures in the top row, the smaller shapes are identical to the larger shape except for their sizes. So Answer A is ruled out. **Therefore the correct answer is C.**

14. At first glance, we see that the pictures in the top row have no curves. So Answer N is ruled out. Next let's count lines. We see that each picture in the top row has six lines. Among the five answer choices, only Answer K has six lines. **So the right answer is K.**

15. Looking carefully at the three pictures in the top row, we notice that Picture One consists of one kind of rectangles and Picture Two consists of another kind of rectangles. Picture Three is a combination of these two types of rectangles. Now let's look at the answer choices. Only Answer A is a combination of these two types of rectangles. **So the right answer is A.**

16. We see that in each of the three pictures in the top row, a shape is partially covered by three identical shapes of another kind. So Answers M and N are ruled out. Next we observe that in each of the pictures in the top row, the three identical shapes are all located at the bottom right corner of the picture. So Answers J and L are ruled out. **So the right answer is K.**

17. This is a counting problem. We observe that in each of the three pictures in the top row, the number of the inner shapes is the same as the number of lines of the outer shape. Examining all five answer choices, only Answer E has this property. **So the right answer is E.**

18. This is a rotation problem. We see that in each of the three pictures in the top row, the small triangle is immediately followed by the large triangle when we rotate the picture clockwise. Now let's look at the answer choices. We see that only Answer L has this property and all the other answer choices are the other way around. **So the right answer is L.**

19. Again this is a rotation problem. We see that in each of the three pictures in the top row, the shorter arrow goes ahead of the longer arrow when we rotate the shape clockwise. Answers B, C, D, and E are not correct because when we rotate them clockwise, we see that it is the longer arrow that goes ahead of the shorter arrow. **So the right answer is A.**

20. Again this is a counting problem. Let's count lines. We notice that in each of the three pictures in the top row, there are in total 12 lines inside the big square. Now let's count the lines of all the answer choices. We see that only Answer K has this property. **So the right answer is K.**

21. We see that each picture in the top row can be drawn without lifting the pencil from the paper or tracing back the lines. Among the five answer choices, only Answer C has this property. **So the right answer is C.** If you would like to know why it's impossible to draw the other answer pictures without lifting the pencil from the paper or tracing back the lines, here is the reason. For the pencil to draw through a vertex of a shape, this vertex must have one line for the pencil to reach it and a different line for the pencil to leave it. So unless this vertex is the starting point or the ending point of the drawing, it must have an even number of lines connecting it to make it possible to draw without lifting the pencil from the paper or tracing back the lines. In other words, for a shape to be drawable without lifting the pencil from the paper or tracing back the lines, it must have at most two vertices with an odd number of lines connecting these vertices. Now let's examine Answers A, B, D, and E. We see that each of them has at least three vertices with an odd number of lines connecting them. So these shapes cannot be drawn without lifting the pencil from the paper or tracing back the lines.

22. First we notice that in each of the three pictures in the top row, the black circles never touch the white circles. So Answers J, K, and M are ruled out. Next we observe that in the top row, the white circles are always connected with each other by lines in between. So Answer N is ruled out. Only Answer L fits all these patterns. **So the right answer is L.**

Closing Words

What? You got all the answers right and filled the bubble form right? Nooooooo!! What will become of me?! Think, think, think...Umm... I got it!! Just you wait little CogAT Cat, I'll get you in SAT! Just wait and see!

All right, Trapdog, let's wait and see! You'll probably fail again! Meanwhile, good luck, CogAT test taker! Remember these tips and you'll do great!!

Disclaimer: The Trapdog is a purely fictitious character. Neither the author nor the publisher thinks that he has anything to do with CogAT test designers or any other standard test designers. Whoever thinks otherwise is exercising his/her imagination.

About the Author

Karen Ge is a student at Kennedy Junior High School in Illinois at the time of publication. She scored a perfect 99 NPR (National Percentile Rank) in each of the three cognitive areas (Verbal, Quantitative, and Nonverbal) on the CogAT Form 7. In her free time, Karen likes to play with her friends, make up stories out of Legos, and practice the violin.